Dan Friedman

HARPERS FERRY

By

Barrie Stavis

Fiction

HOME, SWEET HOME!

THE CHAIN OF COMMAND

Plays

LAMP AT MIDNIGHT

THE MAN WHO NEVER DIED

COAT OF MANY COLORS

REFUGE

HARPERS FERRY

A Play about John Brown

by

BARRIE STAVIS

INTRODUCTION BY TYRONE GUTHRIE

South Brunswick
New York: A. S. Barnes and Company
London: Thomas Yoseloff Ltd

Library of Congress Catalogue Card Number: 67-23982
A. S. Barnes and Co., Inc.
Cranbury, N. J. 08512

Thomas Yoseloff Ltd
108 New Bond Street
London W1Y OQX, England

SBN: 498 06728 9

Printed in the United States of America

Contents

FOR BERNICE, FOR TYRONE GUTHRIE,

AND FOR

DOUGLAS CAMPBELL AND PETER ZEISLER

Introduction

I write as one whose task it will shortly be to stage the first performance of *Harpers Ferry.* It will be the first new play the Minnesota Theatre Company has produced. It tells the story of John Brown, the farmer, who believed so strongly that man must not enslave his fellow man that, against utterly impossible odds, he led a Movement of Violent Protest. The movement was crushed, and John Brown was brought to trial for High Treason.

The judges, in my opinion, could not but find him guilty of the crime of which he was accused; the penalty was death. John Brown was hanged. But his name will live forever.

The play has been included in our classical repertoire because we believe it to be an interpretation of noble and monumental simplicity of a piece of American history, small — almost local in scale, but like many apparently small events, of large symbolical importance.

Harpers Ferry is the name of the little river town in Virginia which housed the Armory and Arsenal which Brown and his tiny band of followers tried to capture in the fall of 1859. Barrie Stavis has found a style splendidly suited to a story which, although the events occurred only a century ago, has already assumed legendary proportions. It is a style which avoids, on the one hand, inflated and self-consciously heroic diction, and, on the other, the flatness and triviality of realistic conversation. Furthermore, the architectural design of the play disregards the conventions of the naturalistic theatre. Even if technical means could be found (and they probably could) of changing from scene to realistic scene without slowing up the play's progress, literal indications of locality would reduce the legendary nature of John Brown's extraordinary exploit to the level of prosaic fact.

Barrie Stavis has adhered to the facts of history as far as they are known — and a great deal is known about events so comparatively recent and so obviously significant. But he has not treated these facts realistically. He has selected and simplified, not with the intention of grinding a moral or political axe, nor to magnify or minimize John Brown's achievement, nor to glorify or denigrate his character; but rather to show that a person of such character cannot, *literally cannot,* act otherwise than as he believes right. It is not maintained that Brown *was* right; nor even that this was an intelligent way to attack the institution of slavery; merely that it was Brown's way; that Brown was a person of heroic stature, of great shrewdness, as shown by the way he mobilized and exploited public opinion in the brief interim between his capture and execution; and that his actions, however complex their unconscious motivation, were untainted in the slightest degree by materialism or self-seeking.

His idealism was pure; he was willing to pay for his mistakes with his life. Few can ever have had a more indisputable right to join the noble army of martyrs.

It is always hard to know whether a play which reads well will also turn out well on the stage. So many things can go wrong! Failure on the stage does not necessarily signify a poor play, any more than success on the stage implies a good one. Success and failure are not a reliable guide to quality. One of the problems of the theatre as a profession is the terrible and necessary importance which attaches itself to success. Therefore, it is the more satisfactory that *Harpers Ferry* is being submited to the judgment of readers, not merely to that of playgoers and their bear-leaders, the theatrical critics. As a rule, publishers wait for a play to be A Success before risking the expense of bringing it out in book-form. I congratulate the publisher of this volume on his courage; I share his confidence in the play's merits.

— Tyrone Guthrie
April, 1967

Preface

John Brown: The Power of the Ethical Imperative

(During October, 1966, I delivered a lecture on John Brown at the Menninger Foundation, Topeka, Kansas. The lecture is published as a companion volume to HARPERS FERRY. The following preface is excerpted from it.)

In 1834, John Brown, then living in Pennsylvania, wrote to his brother in Ohio. This letter is of extreme interest because it is the first time he put into writing a plan to help slaves:

> I have been trying to devise some means whereby I might do something in a practical way for my poor fellow-men who are in bondage, and having fully consulted the feelings of my wife and my three boys, we have agreed to get at least one negro boy or youth, and bring him up as we do our own, viz, give him a good English education, learn him what we can about the history of the world, about business, about general subjects, and, above all, try to teach him the fear of God. We think of three ways to obtain one; First, to try to get some Christian slaveholder to release one to us. Second, to get a free one if no one will let us have one that is a slave. Third, if that does not succeed, we have all agreed to submit to considerable privation in order to buy one. . . .

> Perhaps, we might, under God, in that way do more towards breaking their yoke effectually than in any other. If the young blacks of our country could once become enlightened, it would most assuredly operate on slavery like firing powder confined in rock, and all slaveholders know it well. Witness their heaven-daring laws against teaching blacks. If once the Christians in the free States would set to work in earnest in teaching blacks, the people of the slaveholding States would find themselves constitutionally driven to set about the work of emancipation immediately.

Here we see the shape of John Brown's thinking. He recognized that enforced ignorance was a weapon used very consciously by the South; it was a penal offense to teach a slave to read. He saw education as the lever which could force the slave owner to extend freedom to the slaves; thus, he would get a Negro youth and raise him in his house as one of his own children. The key was to be education and a model school which would encourage others in the North to found similar schools.

This letter was written when the issue of slavery, although sharply debated, did not yet dominate the national scene. Exactly twenty-five years later, in 1859, John Brown made his famous raid on Harpers Ferry. In the intervening years the Fugitive Slave Law had been passed, battles had been fought to bring Kansas Territory into the Union as a free state, the Dred Scott Decision had been handed down by the Supreme Court; the issue had sharpened so that many on both sides knew that they were drawing closer to the impending conflict. By 1859, in fact long before that, John Brown was convinced that the slaveholder would fight to the death to maintain the institution of slavery, because the whole fabric of his society rested on his ownership of property in the shape of human beings. In the 1850's, there were four million slaves in the United States having an average worth of one thousand dollars each; thus, the slave system had an investment of four billion dollars in human property. This investment generated a profit of between 500 million and 750 million dollars a year. (When Lincoln signed the Emancipation Proclamation on January 1, 1863, he effectively stripped the South of four billion dollars in capital, and of one-half to three-quarters of a billion dollars in annual income.) Long before 1859, John Brown had come to realize that education for the slave was not the key; the only way to destroy the system was by the sword.

* * * * * *

In 1850, the Fugitive Slave Law was passed, the North fighting the bill every step of the way. Henrietta Buckmaster, in her superb book on the Underground Railroad and the Abolition Movement, *Let My People Go,* details the provisions of the Fugitive Slave Law:

> The identification of a fugitive slave could be made on the affidavit of a slave catcher without effort to substantiate his word. The fugitive could offer no defense, could not testify for himself. He was not allowed a trial by jury. The fee of the commissioner who settled the case was to be ten dollars if he found for the master and only five dollars if he freed the fugitive. If a Federal agent hampered in any way the seizure of a fugitive he was to be fined a thousand dollars, and if a fugitive escaped, with or without his help, he would be held responsible for the entire value of the slave. Bystanders could be forced to lend a hand if a fugitive tried to escape. And friends, in the underground work, or casual humanitarians, were liable to a fine of a thousand dollars or imprisonment for six months, if they were convicted of passing him on.

In the North, people in all walks of life were outraged and repelled by a law which could force them to help a slave-catcher—doubly so, when the slave-catcher, merely by making out an affidavit, could apprehend any Negro he desired, whether a fugitive slave or a free man. There were slave-catchers who made a thriving business of scouting Northern towns for free Negroes with identifying marks. These slave-catchers would return to the South where a fellow-conspirator used the description supplied by the slave-catcher to swear out an affidavit that such and such a slave had escaped. The slave-catcher, armed with the affidavit, would go back North, swear out a warrant and hire a few bullies to help him apprehend the Negro—really abduct him. No Negro in the North, escaped or free, felt safe, for he never knew when he would be pounced upon and abducted into a life of slavery.

John Brown's practical response to the Fugitive Slave Law was to form the "League of the Gileadites." This was an organization of Negroes and white friends, designed to resist the Fugitive Slave Law. The program for the League, written by John Brown, expounds the doctrine of the commando raid:

> Should one of your number be arrested, you must collect together as quickly as possible, so as to outnumber your adversaries. . . . Let no able-bodied man appear on the ground unequipped, or with his weapons exposed to view. . . . Do not delay one moment after you are ready. . . . Let the first blow be the signal for all to engage. . . . By going about your business quietly, you will get the job disposed of before the number that an uproar would bring together can collect; and you will have the advantage of those who come out against you, for they will be wholly unprepared with either equipments or matured plans; all with them will be confusion and terror.

John Brown, and all those who resisted the Fugitive Slave Law, were, of course, breaking the law of the land. In this, they were following the position of Henry Thoreau, who, in turn, was in the direct tradition of William Godwin. In 1793, William Godwin wrote his *Enquiry Concerning Political Justice and Its Influence on Morals and Happiness* wherein he contends that too often moral law is disregarded in favor of political expediency, with a resultant economic advantage to a select few. Since moral law is fundamental and superior to the laws of government, every citizen not only may, but must set aside the law of the state if need be. It is his *duty* to follow the higher law of morality.

This rejection of an unjust man-made law, this demand that every citizen declare and render allegiance to the higher law of morality, is precisely what Henry Thoreau advocated in his *Civil Disobedience,* published in 1849. Thoreau went to jail rather than have any part of the war against Mexico which would add slave territory to the United States. Said Thoreau in his *Civil Disobedience:*

It is not desirable to cultivate a respect for the law, so much as for the right. . . . How does it become a man to behave toward this American government today? I answer, that he cannot without disgrace be associated with it. I cannot for an instant recognize that political organization as *my* government which is the *slave's* government also. . . . [If the law] is of such a nature that it requires you to be an agent of injustice to another, then, I say, break the law. Let your life be a counter-friction to stop the machine.

This position was shared by thousands of citizens of conscience who disobeyed the Fugitive Slave Law as a matter of principle. This is an American tradition which did not die with the Abolitionist Era. During the early 1900's in the West, the Industrial Workers of the World, the I.W.W., resorted to mass civil disobedience in their Free Speech fights in order to protect the rights of free speech. In our own time, Mahatma Gandhi acknowledged his indebtedness to Thoreau when Gandhi was evolving his strategy to achieve independence for India—passive mass resistance by so large a segment of the population that the machinery of the courts must break down under the impact. The present day civil-liberties struggle in the United States, where the strategy is non-violent mass resistance, is in this same tradition.

Thoreau who, in 1849, advocated *passive resistance* to a morally corrupt government, only ten years later, in 1859, shifted his position so drastically that he embraced the action of John Brown and the raid on Harpers Ferry. During the intervening years, he had come to learn that under given conditions it becomes necessary to transform a doctrine into a deed. He considered John Brown *the* great man of the century, a man who perfectly synthesized ethic with action. Thoreau's diary is replete with the anguish he felt as John Brown lay in prison. To Thoreau belongs the distinction of being the first American to make a public statement in defense of John Brown. He knocked at doors, spoke to neighbors on the streets, invited them to come to Concord Town Hall to hear what he had to say.

Preface

In his address delivered before the citizens of Concord on October 30, 1859, during the very days that John Brown's trial was taking place in Charles Town, Virginia, Thoreau said:

> He did not value his life in comparison with ideal things. He did not recognize unjust human laws, but resisted them as he was bid. For once we are lifted out of the trivialness and dust of politics into the region of truth and manhood. No man in America has ever stood up so persistently and effectively for the dignity of human nature, knowing himself for a man, and the equal of any and all governments. In that sense he was the most American of us all. . . .
>
> It was his peculiar doctrine that a man has a perfect right to interfere by force with the slaveholder, in order to rescue the slave. I agree with him. . . . I shall not be forward to think him mistaken in his method who quickest succeeds to liberate the slave. . . . I think that for once the Sharps rifles and the revolvers were employed in a righteous cause. The tools were in the hands of one who could use them.

This belief, "that a man has a perfect right to interfere by force with the slaveholder, in order to rescue the slave," was also shared by Rev. Theodore Parker, famous Unitarian minister and orator. Parker's position stemmed, as did John Brown's, from the fact that both considered slavery to be a state of war in which a powerful majority exercised violence against a defenseless minority. Further, this institutionalized violence was sanctioned by the state. Slaves, therefore, were prisoners of war; in such a war, the minority has the right to avail itself of any and all means to achieve its rightful freedom. Parker forcefully expressed this concept in a letter to Francis Jackson, lawyer and powerful Abolitionist. The letter was written from Rome, dated November 24, 1859, eight days before the scheduled hanging of John Brown; Jackson received it after the hanging. In it Parker said:

> If you were attacked by a wolf, I should not only have a *right* to aid you in getting rid of the enemy, but it would be my *duty* to help you in proportion to my power. If it were a *murderer,* and not a wolf who attacked you, the duty would be still the same. Suppose it is not a murderer who would kill

you, but a *kidnapper* who would enslave, does that make it less my duty to help you out of the hands of your enemy? Suppose it is not a kidnapper who would make you a bondman, but a *slaveholder* who would keep you one, does that remove my obligation to help you?

Parker clearly foresaw the Civil War. In the same letter he told Jackson:

The American people will have to march to rather severe music, I think, and it is better for them to face it in season. A few years ago it did not seem difficult first to check slavery, and then to end it without any bloodshed. I think this cannot be done now, nor ever in the future. All the great charters of HUMANITY have been writ in blood. I once hoped that of American Democracy would be engrossed in less costly ink; but it is plain, now, that our pilgrimage must lead through a Red Sea, wherein many a Pharaoh will go under and perish. Alas! that we are not wise enough to be just, or just enough to be wise, and so gain much at small cost!

* * * * * *

John Brown's raid on Harpers Ferry was at first spectacularly successful; then the situation turned against him and his men. They were pinned down by superior forces; the raid was smashed. Many of his men were killed, including two of his sons; others were captured. John Brown, himself wounded, on trial for his life, his raid turned to ashes, began to realize that if he no longer could carry on the battle against slavery with the sword, he still had the word. The word, too, as well as the sword, had the capacity to persuade. As the man of action, he had sought to reach the committed; now by his word he reached the uncommitted. During his trial and when in prison, his impassioned words shook the nation.

In addition to a literary outpouring by Thoreau, Emerson, Parker, Wendell Phillips and many others, there were poems by Walt Whitman, Herman Melville, William Dean Howells, Louisa May Alcott, John Greenleaf Whittier, Bronson Alcott, and others too. Articles were in the press; speeches were given in town halls. Many a sermon was delivered from a Sunday pulpit by the most influential ministers of the day. These sermons were subsequently printed in booklet form. Sold in the thousands, they found their way into many homes where they were avidly read.

At the conclusion of the trial, the judge asked John Brown if he had anything to say before sentence was pronounced. John Brown, still suffering from wounds received when captured at Harpers Ferry, began with the customary, "I have, may it please the Court, a few words to say." And then followed a speech, which, although not taught in the schools, is an American prose classic. When Ralph Waldo Emerson delivered a funeral address for Abraham Lincoln, he compared John Brown's address to the court with Lincoln's at Gettysburg. Said Emerson, "His brief speech at Gettysburg will not easily be surpassed by words on any recorded occasion. This and one other American speech, that of John Brown to the court that tried him and a part of Kossuth's speech at Birmingham, can only be compared with each other, and with no fourth." Here, in part, is John Brown's address to the court:

> Had I interfered in the manner which I admit . . . had I so interfered in behalf of the rich, the powerful, the intelligent, the so-called great, or in behalf of any of their friends, either father, mother, brother, sister, wife or children, or any of that class, and suffered and sacrificed what I have in this interference, it would have been all right. Every man in this court would have deemed it an act worthy of reward rather than punishment.
>
> This Court acknowledges, too, as I suppose, the validity of the law of God. I see a book kissed, which I suppose to be the Bible, or at least the New Testament, which teaches me that all things whatsoever I would that men should do to me, I should do even so to them. It teaches me, further, to remember them that are in bonds as bound with them. I endeavored to act up to that instruction. I say I am yet too young to understand that God is any respecter of persons. I believe that to have interfered as I have done, as I always have freely admitted I have done, in behalf of His despised poor, I did no wrong, but right. Now, if it is deemed necessary that I should forfeit my life for the furtherance of the ends of justice, and mingle my blood further with the blood of my children and with the blood of millions in this slave country whose rights are disregarded by wicked, cruel and unjust enactments, I submit. So let it be done.

* * * * * *

PREFACE

Year of meteors! brooding year!
I would bind in words retrospective some of your deeds and signs, . . .
I would sing how an old man, tall, with white hair, mounted the scaffold in
 Virginia,
(I was at hand, silent I stood with teeth shut close, I watch'd,
I stood very near you old man when cool and indifferent, but trembling with
 age and your unheal'd wounds, you mounted the scaffold;)

Walt Whitman
Year of Meteors
(1859-60)

* * * * * *

He was hanged on December 2, 1859, and his body was brought to his home in North Elba, high in the Adirondack Mountains of New York, for burial. As the train bearing his body moved East and then North, solemn church bells rang out. The bells rang in Ravenna, in Cleveland, in Philadelphia, in New York, in Rochester, in Syracuse, in Vergennes, in Fitchburg, in Plymouth, in Concord, Massachusetts, and in Concord, New Hampshire, in New Bedford, in Manchester, in Providence, in Albany, in Troy, in Rutland and in Westport. The funeral cortege stayed overnight at Elizabethtown; the coffin was reverently placed in the courthouse and a guard of honor was stationed through the night.

He was buried on December 8, 1859. He had asked to be buried in the shadow of a great granite rock, and he was so buried. His body in the shadow of the great granite rock; the granite rock in the shadow of the great granite White Mountain which he loved so dear. The granite thrust of his will, the granite thrust of his Old Testament conscience, the granite of the mountains, all were now one.

From this tiny village, North Elba, situated high in the Adirondack Mountains, six men were lost by the raid on Harpers Ferry, including two sons of John and Mary Brown. All six men were intertwined into one family, relatives either by blood or by marriage. The women of these intertwined families suffered grievous loss. They stood around the open grave of John Brown and listened to Wendell Phillips, orator and Abolitionist:

He has abolished slavery in Virginia. . . . History will date Virginia Emancipation from Harpers Ferry. True, the slave is still there. So, when the tempest uproots a pine on your hills, it looks green for months,—a year or two. Still, it is timber, not a tree. John Brown has loosened the roots of the slave system; it only breathes,—it does not live,—hereafter.

Seventeen months after the hanging of John Brown, the first shots were fired at Fort Sumter, ushering in the Civil War. John Brown's apocalyptic statement the morning of his hanging, "I, John Brown, am now quite certain that the crimes of this guilty land will never be purged away but with blood," were to become a tragic reality.

March, 1967 BARRIE STAVIS
New York City

Acknowledgments

HARPERS FERRY has been many years in the writing. Along the road, scores of people have helped me bring the play into final shape. Frequently, the discussions were lengthy; at other times, a single sentence would illuminate for me an area which needed work.

I well remember a comment my cousin, Esther Stavis, made after she had read one of the earlier drafts. "John Brown is not God-driven enough." This sentence was always with me as I worked on subsequent drafts. Michael Langham wrote, "My only reservation about it [the play] is that I wish it could be more economical in words. I think this would make the ammunition of the speeches of a greater calibre." Immediately I set out to re-examine every speech, cutting, pruning, highlighting, rather than letting the play be obscured in a uniform welter of words. I shall not soon forget Sir Tyrone Guthrie's marvelous four-page letter on August 13, 1960, written shortly after he had read the first completed draft of the play. His letter began: "I've read the play and offer you respectful congratulations on what I really do think a noble and moving piece of work." Then, he got down to the important business at hand: "The second act—the battle of Harpers Ferry—is far more suited to the film than to the stage. You have been ingenious but, even so, lots of these short scenes of chasing, shooting, wrestling, etc. would be *very* hard to stage and could *very* easily be ridiculous. None of this is the *sort* of thing for which the theatre is suited. If Shakespeare could leave the battle of Agincourt out of HENRY V, I don't see why you can't leave the battle out of your play." Some thirty pages of battle scenes were lopped off the script! But of greater importance than the cutting itself, Sir Tyrone's insightful comment gave *me* insight into the further shaping of the material.

First and foremost, my indebtedness to Sir Tyrone Guthrie, generous and dear friend, brilliant man of the theatre. Then comes the invaluable assistance of Adelaide Bean, Stephen Gray, B. J. Whiting. I will never be able to repay their penetrating criticism and their endless patience.

Then, a host of people who, in one way or another, helped me bring this play to its conclusion: Dr. Alexander Thomas, Dr. Stella Chess, Prof. Christian H. Moe, Prof. Mordecai Gorelik, Dr. Sam Smiley, Dr. Dudley Thomas, Rev. Charles H. King, Jr., Dr. Herbert Aptheker, the late Dr. Emil Conason, the late Dr. W. E. B. DuBois, Prof. John F. Matthews, Douglas Campbell, Michael Langham, Dr. Annette T. Rubinstein, Jean Gascon, Lily Turner, Boris Tumarin, Berta Tumarin, Romaire Bearden, Morton Stavis, Esther Stavis, Benedict Stavis, George Freedley, Alice Childress, Dr. Allan Lewis, Arthur Levine, Howard N. Meyer, Boyd B. Stutler, Alex Schlichting, James de B. Domville, Fred Hellerman, Gilbert Rathbun, Dr. Jere C. Mickel, Ellie Weiss. A special word of friendship and gratitude to Joseph K. Reichbart, counselor and guide. And, finally, my talented wife, Bernice, whose wit and perspective are combined with rare theatrical and literary judgment.

My deep thanks to all of you.

B. S.

Production Notes

THE DESIGN OF THE SET. The set is to be extremely simple; the play is to be performed on a stage consisting of open playing areas. These playing areas can be suggested by platforms, or levels of different heights situated in various parts of the stage. In one scene, a level or platform can be used as the farmhouse; in another scene a different level or platform can be used as the Armory; another as the courtroom; still another as the prison cell; and so forth. . . . There is to be no pause between scenes. The instant a scene is finished, the next scene is to begin. In fact, where possible, overlapping is desirable. The play has been written in this form to achieve a continuous flow of action and time. The simplicity of the set will help to provide fluidity, thereby enriching the action and impact. . . . When indicated, two scenes of different playing areas are to be played against each other in counterpoint and then blend when a character from one scene moves across the stage into the other scene.

LIGHTING. Lighting plays an important part in the production of this play. Scene changes will be indicated by the use of lights which will dim down on one area and come up on another. Lights will serve to spot one part of the stage when the other is not in use.

The play was presented by the Minnesota Theatre Company at the Tyrone Guthrie Theatre in Minneapolis, Minnesota. It was first performed on June 3, 1967.

Cast of Characters

John Brown	Edward Binns
Mary Brown	Katherine Squire
Martha Brown	Melody Greer
Soldiers in John Brown's Army:	
Oliver Brown	Michael Moriarty
Watson Brown	Jan Pearce
Owen Brown	James Wallace
John Kagi	Len Cariou
Aaron Stevens	Philip Kerr
Dangerfield Newby	Adolph Caesar
Charles Tidd	James J. Lawless
William Leeman	Joseph Klimowski
William Thompson	Richard Ramos
Osborn Anderson	George Spelvin
Lewis Leary	J. Walter Smith
John Copeland	Granville Van Dusen
Stewart Taylor	Michael Pierce
Jeremiah Anderson	William Greene

Cast of Characters

Barclay Coppoc	Ronald Boulden
Edwin Coppoc	Travis Lockhart
John Cook	Earl Boen
Shields Green	Glynn Turman
Mrs. Huffmaster	Grace Keagy
Frederick Douglass	Fred Pinkard
A Deer-hunter	Richard Ramos
Col. Lewis Washington	Robert Pastene
A Prisoner	Robert Skloot
Andrew Kitzmiller	George Mitchell
Dr. John Starry	Paul Ballantyne
Col. Robert E. Lee	Earl Boen
Lt. J. E. B. Stuart	Philip Kerr
Gov. Henry A. Wise	James Wallace
Andrew Hunter	Lee Richardson
A Newspaper Reporter	Michael Pierce
Sen. J. M. Mason	John Lewin
Terence Byrne	James J. Lawless
Judge Parker	George Mitchell
Lawson Botts	Philip Kerr
Thomas Dennis	Michael Moriarty
Capt. John Avis	Paul Ballantyne

Prisoners, Marines, Reporter, Court Attendants, etc.: James Alexander, Ronald Boulden, Jon Cranney, David Flaten, Frederick Gaines, Robert Lanchester, Robert Skloot.

Designed by
Lewis Brown

Technical Director: Richard Borgen
Production Stage Manager: Rex Partington
Stage Managers: Gordon Smith and Milt Commons

Directed by TYRONE GUTHRIE

The action of the play takes place in and around Harpers Ferry, Virginia, during October, November, and December, 1859.

HARPERS FERRY

No voice is wholly lost; not even
the lone cry in the desert.

Act I

A day in October, 1859.
The general living room of the Kennedy Farmhouse in the hills of Maryland, about five miles away from Harpers Ferry, Virginia. It is a small room. A number of crates and packing boxes are piled on one side.
Time is compressed. There are to be appropriate light changes.
There are sixteen people present. Two are women: Mary Brown (age 48) and Martha Brown (age 17). The names of the fourteen men in alphabetical order are:

Jeremiah Goldsmith Anderson	*Age 27*
Osborn Perry Anderson	*Age 29*
(no relation to Jeremiah Anderson)	
John Brown	*Age 59*
Oliver Brown	*Age 20*
Watson Brown	*Age 24*
John Anthony Copeland	*Age 25*
John Henry Kagi	*Age 24*
Lewis Sheridan Leary	*Age 25*
Dangerfield Newby	*Age 44*
Aaron Dwight Stevens	*Age 29*
Stewart Taylor	*Age 23*
William Leeman	*Age 20*
William Thompson	*Age 26*
Charles Plummer Tidd	*Age 25*

Newby and Leary are Mulattoes, Osborn Anderson and Copeland are full-blooded Negroes; the others are white. They are active, strong, restless and are beginning to show the strains of their confinement. Kagi is second in command, Stevens is third in command.

Mary and Martha are busy preparing breakfast. The men are whittling, reading, playing cards and checkers. John Brown goes to one side of the stage and looks off in the direction of Harpers Ferry.

JOHN BROWN. Harpers Ferry. There she lies—five miles away. A small and quiet town no different from a thousand other towns across this land. No different except for your Armory and your Arsenal, your guns and your ammunition. When we have finished with our work, oh Harpers Ferry, we shall have made a great noise, thunder which will enter every home and shake every wall to its foundation. Sleep, oh Harpers Ferry, sleep. You have slept in peace this night; continue to sleep in peace every night, until that particular night when we are ready for you.

MARY. Breakfast.

JOHN BROWN. Martha, take up your watch. (*Martha gets knitting and sits in playing area designating porch. She is half-way through knitting a man's long gray scarf. As she knits, she watches the road.*)

MARY. On today's bill of fare we have onions and bacon, bread and coffee.

TIDD. (*In a low voice, wryly repeats after Mary, then says.*) We know the menu. We've had the same thing for the last three weeks.

MARY. I'm ready for the first group. (*John Brown, Stevens, Osborn Anderson, Leeman, Thompson, Copeland and Jeremiah Anderson take plate, cup, spoon and fork and line up. Mary serves them. They sit with bowed heads, the untouched food before them. Tidd and Newby at their checker board and Watson and Leary at their card game wait with bowed heads. Martha stops knitting and bows her head, but one eye is on the road.*)

JOHN BROWN. I will pray. (*He prays standing very erect, head held high.*)

I am here, oh Lord God. Use me!
Lord, God of Hosts, pour forth Thy wrath upon the slaveholder. Pour Thy wrath upon them, Lord, God of Judgment, for they violate Thy most sacred precept by taking men and women with divine souls and transforming them into property.
For this, Lord, God of Judgment, let thorns grow instead of wheat; let them hunger so that they feed on their own flesh; let the salted sweat from their brow be their only drink.
Evil burns in this land; the earth is given over into the hands of the wicked. They have eaten of their food themselves alone, and the slave and the fatherless have not eaten thereof.
Lord, God of Judgment, touch bone and flesh. As the sparks fly upward and are consumed and disappear, so let it be with the slaveholder, Lord, God of Judgment, Lord of Wrath.
The slave must be freed. I know that it must be done, and I know that it must be done now, and I know that I am called upon to do it. For if not now, when? If not I, who?
Lord, help me to comfort all that mourn.
Lord, God, I swear to you the work will soon begin.
JEREMIAH ANDERSON. You are God's servant. Why do you not bend the knee when you utter such an earnest prayer?
JOHN BROWN. I cannot bend the knee. I must pray standing. It is true that I am God's servant; it is equally true that I am God's partner. God did not say to me, "Gather your Army and go to Harpers Ferry and there launch your attack." If God were so specific, then I would indeed be only a servant and should bend the knee. But that is not the situation. A task has been assigned me by God—but the details are left to me. It was I who toiled on this plan for twenty years. It was I who selected Harpers Ferry as the point of attack. In this sense I am God's partner. And since I am God's partner, how can I bend the knee?
JEREMIAH ANDERSON. But what of your defects and sins? Should you bend the knee for those?
JOHN BROWN. Have I defects? Yes. Sins? Yes. But I am on the

side of God and freedom. And this fact and this power will carry me through. . . . God and I have a passion to make men free and this is the hour in history in which it will be done. (*The men at the table begin to eat. The others resume their activities: Tidd and Newby play checkers; Watson and Leary play cards; Oliver reads a book; Taylor picks up a notebook and pencil.*)

NEWBY. What is the score?

TIDD. 328 to 142. My favor.

NEWBY. We were even at one point.

TIDD. A long time ago. We play ten games a day and you've won only half a dozen games this past week.

NEWBY. I'll hit a streak. We'll be even.

TIDD. Never.

LEARY. (*Taking in some cards.*) And four is nine. That gives me the game.

WATSON. (*Marking it on the sheet of paper.*) Making it 6,283 to 4,971. Your favor.

LEARY. I've mastered your style of playing. Change your attack once in a while. Confuse me.

TAYLOR. (*Approaches Oliver, pencil poised over notebook.*) Please read aloud to me.

OLIVER. (*Reads.*) "There is a time in every man's education when he arrives at the conviction that envy is ignorance; that imitation is suicide; that he must take himself for better or worse as his portion." (*Taylor reads passage back, though somewhat haltingly.*) Splendid.

TAYLOR. Too slow. I need more practice. Go on reading.

OLIVER. (*Reads.*) "Though the wide universe is full of good, no kernel of nourishing corn can come to him but through—"

MARY. I'm ready for the second group. (*Oliver sees that some of the men have moved away from table. He touches Taylor and points to empty places. They get food and eat hungrily. Meanwhile, Thompson and Osborn Anderson begin a checker game; Leeman and Jeremiah Anderson begin a card game; Stevens and Copeland also play cards. Later, when the second shift finish their meal, they engage in card and checker playing, reading; one man whittles, another man works on a puzzle.)*

MARY. (*Serving Tidd. He has no cup of coffee. She tries to give him one.*) Let me give you some coffee.

TIDD. Do not tempt me to break my resolutions.

MARY. There is not enough food and the little there is, is boring in its repetition. Take some coffee.

TIDD. For two years I have not touched coffee or tea. If by my self-denial I can atone for the sin of this land, then I am content. (*He goes without coffee.*)

JEREMIAH ANDERSON. If we scrape the grease off these cards we'd have enough to fry eggs in.

LEEMAN. If we had the eggs. (*He laughs over his own joke. The others look on in stony silence.*)

JEREMIAH ANDERSON. They're so dirty I can hardly read the numbers.

LEEMAN. Then how do you know what you've got in your hand?

JEREMIAH ANDERSON. By the grease and dirt marks on each card.

LEEMAN. That's my special secret.

JEREMIAH ANDERSON. The special secret of everyone in this farmhouse.

LEEMAN. If you know the markings, then you know what I've got in my hand.

JEREMIAH ANDERSON. I could if I wanted to—but I turn my eyes away when I deal—as you do when you deal. Play.

COPELAND. Who has a good subject for today's debate?

LEARY. Resolved, Cromwell was a greater general than Napoleon.

KAGI. We have debated that subject three times in the last five days; squeezed it dry. No Napoleon; no Cromwell.

TIDD. (*To Mary.*) My boredom weighs heavily. Teach me to iron.

LEEMAN. Resolved that the love a man and woman give each other freely without benefit of marriage is more true, and therefore more

virtuous, than the enforced and methodical connubiality of marriage.
OLIVER. We can't debate that proposition.
LEEMAN. Why not? It's a subject which interests every person on the threshold of life.
OLIVER. There's no one here with the other kind of experience to debate it.
LEEMAN. (*Disappointed.*) Oh.
TIDD. Are we to have nothing but cards and checkers and his shorthand today? (*Points at Taylor who is taking shorthand notes of the general conversation.*)
NEWBY. (*As he talks, the others cease their activities and listen attentively.*) I couldn't sleep last night. I found myself thinking of my father, that good white man from Scotland, who loved a black slave woman, my mother, who bought her freedom, married her, had children by her, and who took his black and beautiful wife and the Mulatto children she bore him, and set them free. I am free. . . . And I thought of my wife, a slave, and of my seven children. No. They are the property of Jesse Jennings of Warington, Virginia, slave-master. I thought of many things last night, but of these two, my father and my wife, my thoughts were the deepest. And I thought how there is both good and evil in the world and I asked myself: "Who is responsible for good? God? Then who is responsible for evil? Man?" But man is God's child. God cannot be evil, yet undoubtedly His children are. But how can God not be evil if He has the power to prevent it, yet allows evil to flourish? . . . My soul cries out in the need to believe in God's goodness. Yet I am troubled and perhaps there are others who are troubled.
STEVENS. An interesting subject for debate.
NEWBY. So I propose the following: Resolved—God is good, for God does not do unto Man the evil which Man does unto himself.
KAGI. The proposition has a flaw—
TIDD. (*Moves to Kagi, leaving iron on shirt. Mary pulls iron off shirt.*) How so? . . . Unless you intend to advance the argument—
KAGI. It rests on the fundamental assumption that there is a God.

As an agnostic, I cannot accept such an assumption.
OLIVER. I would like to participate. As I see it, the issue revolves around the question of—
TIDD. Hold it. Save it for the debate.
KAGI. I take the position that—
TIDD. Save your ammunition for the debate.
JOHN BROWN. Why debate this subject? There are so many others. This subject displeases me greatly.
KAGI. Captain, we are united in this farmhouse on one issue only—that slavery must be abolished. We are not united regarding the nature or even the existence of God. Some of us do not have the answers to this life, much less those of heaven and hell, as firmly in our understanding as you. We respect your certainty; please respect our inquiry. And so, with your permission or without it, we will debate in this farmhouse on all manner of things except on one issue, the necessity to strike the slaveholding power on its own soil.
JOHN BROWN. You are right.
KAGI. (*To all.*) I take the position that God is evil. (*To Tidd.*) Will you join me?
TIDD. (*Who is at the ironing board.*) I devote today to the useful pursuit of learning how to iron.
OLIVER. (*To Newby.*) Will you join me?
NEWBY. I am not skillful enough.
OLIVER. But it was you who raised the proposition.
NEWBY. That doesn't mean that I can debate it. I prefer to listen.
STEVENS (*To Newby.*) Will you be chairman?
NEWBY. Thank you. I will.
OLIVER. (*To Stevens.*) Will you be my partner?
STEVENS. (*Nods, pointing to Kagi.*) I think we can give him a few licks.
KAGI. (*To Copeland.*) Will you join me?
COPELAND. I disagree with your position.
KAGI. (*To Taylor.*) Will you join me?
TAYLOR. My conscience would not allow me to participate on your

side—even as an intellectual exercise.

KAGI. Who in this farmhouse will be my partner? (*His disappointment is obvious.*) A pity Owen hasn't returned.

MARTHA. He would have joined you with pleasure.

KAGI. No one? (*Silence.*) Very well, I shall defend the position single-handed.

MARTHA. Our horse and wagon is coming. It is Owen.

JOHN BROWN. Is he alone?

MARTHA. I can't tell. The wagon is covered.

OWEN BROWN'S VOICE. Hello. Martha. Hello. All is well. (*Owen Brown, age 32, enters followed by Barclay Coppoc, age 20, and Edwin Coppoc, age 24. They are carrying a barrel.*)

BARCLAY COPPOC. Easy. Easy.

JEREMIAH ANDERSON. You handle it as though there were eggs in it.

BARCLAY COPPOC. That's exactly what's in it.

MARY. A feast. Eggs for supper. I'll make them any way you like. Fried, boiled, scrambled, poached. Place your order with the chef.

OWEN. I was able to buy a barrel of eggs on the way. Very cheap. (*The barrel is placed on the floor.*)

BARCLAY COPPOC. Captain Brown!

JOHN BROWN. Welcome, Barclay.

BARCLAY COPPOC. I've brought my older brother along. He's been leading too sheltered a life.

JOHN BROWN. Welcome, Edwin. Barclay, I am very happy to have you with us. Welcome to this farmhouse.

BARCLAY COPPOC. (*Greeting the men he knows.*) Aaron, Oliver, Watson, John Henry.

SEVERAL. Welcome, Barclay. And welcome, Edwin.

OWEN. (*To Newby.*) This letter came through the underground.

NEWBY. Thank you. (*He goes to one side and begins to read it. Until indicated, he remains there, quiet and unmoving.*)

OWEN. Letters for you. (*Owen gives letters to John Brown.*)

JOHN BROWN. We expected you before daylight.

OWEN. The road patrols were active. It is getting more difficult to get through, Father. Every trip increases our chance of discovery.
EDWIN COPPOC. Where are the other men?
KAGI. There will be 18 men coming from Kansas and 12 from the East. And 50 men coming down from Canada.
JOHN BROWN. The men from Canada will be escaped slaves, all recruited by Harriet Tubman. She herself helped most of them to escape and now she will be bringing them back into slave territory to help their brothers win freedom. (*John Brown moves to one side and begins reading the letters.*)
COPELAND. I saw her last year at Oberlin. She had just returned from the South running off twenty-two slaves. She was very tired.
EDWIN COPPOC. Where do we sleep?
KAGI. In the attic.
COPELAND. Let me show you to our palatial quarters. (*Copeland and Edwin Coppoc go up.*)
OSBORN ANDERSON. (*To Barclay Coppoc.*) Are you a good checker player?
BARCLAY COPPOC. It depends on who my opponent is.
THOMPSON. If you and your brother play checkers, we can have an excellent tournament.
LEEMAN. Don't listen to those dull checker players. Join the card players.
OSBORN ANDERSON. We promise you congenial company, stimulation. Join the checker players.
LEEMAN. Their promises are as false as the promises of the whores of Babylon. Join the card players.
BARCLAY COPPOC. Let me eat first, then I'll decide. (*Goes and eats.*)
KAGI. Owen, I want you to be my partner in today's debate. (*John Brown looks up from reading his letters, a frown on his face.*)
OWEN. What's the proposition?
KAGI. God is good, for God does not do unto Man the evil which Man does unto himself. Oliver and Stevens are for the proposition.

I take the position that either God is evil or His powers are limited—a weak, ineffectual sort of God. Will you join me?

OWEN. I'm your man. (*To John Brown, with a sardonic undertone.*) Does it distress you, Father, that I debate this subject?

JOHN BROWN. It will grieve me sorely to hear you speak against God—worse, debate His existence. But speak you will—and must—in the society of this farmhouse. (*He turns his back on Owen.*)

KAGI. Owen, my lad, do you see the opportunities in this debate?

OWEN. If we stay in this farmhouse long enough we'll convert them all into agnostics.

KAGI. (*To Oliver and Stevens.*) Give us a minute to work up our argument. (*The debaters pair off to confer privately.*)

MARY. (*Moving close to John Brown.*) You grieve too sorely.

JOHN BROWN. I have given my permission. What else have I to do?

MARY. Your permission in words—but your spirit is hard against it.

JOHN BROWN. He is my son—and he does this to gall me.

MARY. He is a man. He has a right to his opinion.

JOHN BROWN. To spite me. His hand is against God.

MARY. He has given his whole love to God—and given full proof of it. If he did not love God, he would not be with you in this farmhouse preparing to attack Harpers Ferry. . . . What news in those letters?

JOHN BROWN. It is bad news. Very bad.

MARY. Can you tell me?

JOHN BROWN. There is no time. Not now.

MARY. What will you do?

JOHN BROWN. I don't know yet. (*Mary goes back to ironing board and continues to instruct Tidd. Edwin Coppoc and Copeland return from attic.*)

EDWIN COPPOC. (*Sober and deflated.*) It is a very small attic.

TIDD. We sleep there and we hide there when people are near about.

LEEMAN. There is a Mrs. Huffmaster with her six little children.

TIDD. Six little devils.

KAGI. Six monsters.

LEEMAN. She works a vegetable patch right across the road. She comes in once, twice a day, and nobody knows when it's going to be.

TIDD. And each time we must rush into the attic. Within one week, you will dream of the time you will be able to get your hands around her scrawny neck and twist it and twist it and twist it— (*His voice has risen to a loud cry; others have joined in on the "and twist it".*)

MARTHA. Lower your voices.

TIDD. (*No break, but in a lower voice.*) —and twist it until it can be twisted no more.

LEEMAN. That's exactly what I dreamed last night.

OWEN. Our side is ready. Who's to be chairman?

KAGI. Newby, are you ready?

NEWBY. I will not be chairman.

KAGI. You agreed to, a few minutes ago.

NEWBY. I have changed my mind. (*Silence as everyone looks up.*)

KAGI. (*To Copeland.*) Will you chair?

COPELAND. I will. (*Goes to center of room.*) Ladies and gentlemen, there is no need to introduce our distinguished debaters. Their fame has reached from one end of this room to the other. So, without further ado, let us commence.

OLIVER. Mr. Chairman, ladies and gentlemen. God is good, for God does not do unto Man the evil Man does unto himself. Yet there is evil in the world and at first glance it would appear that God is responsible since God is all-powerful and can—

NEWBY. (*Holding the letter in his hand, comes forward and cries out.*) You stand and you sit, you sit and you stand, and you debate about God's goodness and God's evil, man's goodness and man's evil. We debate about Cromwell and Napoleon. And we do this every day of the week. How long are we going to stand and sit, debate and debate? Harpers Ferry—gateway to the South—sits—waiting.

MARTHA. Lower your voice.

NEWBY. (*Lowers his voice and continues fiercely.*) Four million slaves anguish for the day of liberation.

TIDD. The letter. See what it says.

OWEN. It's from his wife.

MARY. (*Goes to Newby, disengaging the letter from his hand.*) Please, my friend.

NEWBY. My wife and seven children are waiting for liberation. How much time is left before it happens to them?

MARY. (*Reading letter.*) "Our little boy has just begun to crawl. I hold out my hand and he comes to me. But even the comfort of our little boy cannot still my terror. My master is selling off some of his slaves and the children and I are part of the sale. I beg you, come and buy our freedom. If you do not get us, somebody else will."

NEWBY. "Come and buy our freedom." On the auction block the price of my wife is a thousand dollars. My children would bring an average price of six hundred dollars. Total 5200 dollars. "Come and buy our freedom." Come and buy! All I need is 5200 dollars— (*Takes a rifle in his hands.*) —or a rifle . . . Captain, I cannot wait any longer. My wife and children cannot wait any longer. . . . Her master was pleased when I came to visit my wife because out of our love we have produced riches for him. Yes. Yes. He was pleased to see me when I came to visit my wife, but will he be glad to see me now? I will buy my wife and children not with gold, but with the blood of her master.

MARTHA. (*Toward the end of Newby's speech, Martha begins with apparent casualness, but becomes increasingly urgent.*) Pay attention. . . . Pay attention. . . . Mrs. Huffmaster. . . . Up into the attic. . . . Mrs. Huffmaster. . . . Up into the attic. . . . Into the attic. . . . The attic. (*John Brown is the first to hear the warning. He signals the men to move toward attic. With well-rehearsed speed and precision, they grab cards, checkers, every vestige of their presence. Kagi and others attempt to draw Newby into attic, but he throws them off. They rush into attic leaving him there. Everyone is off except Mary, Martha, Oliver, Owen, John Brown and Newby. At the final instant before discovery, Newby realizes what is about to happen. He casts a frantic glance toward the attic, but it is too late for him to get there. He whispers urgently to Oliver, who is closest to him.*)

NEWBY. Catch! (*He tosses the rifle to Oliver. Owen rushes to Oliver's side and they act as though absorbed in cleaning it. Newby turns to John Brown and acts out the part of the humble Negro slave or servant, subservient, head bent.*)

MRS. HUFFMASTER. (*It is a formality, for she is already in.*) Hello, may I come in? (*Calls out to her children in a flat, dispassionate voice.*) Stop pulling hair out of that horse's tail. He needs every bit of it against the flies. (*Pointing to Newby.*) Whose is he?

NEWBY. I am finished, Master. What shall I do next?

JOHN BROWN. The wood needs chopping. I told you that this morning.

NEWBY. Yes, sir, you did. Excuse me, sir.

MARY. Take him out and show him where to stack the wood after chopping it. . . . And now that you've finished cleaning your rifle, why don't you leave us womenfolk by ourselves?

JOHN BROWN. Excuse me, ma'am. (*To Newby.*) Git along, boy. Git!

NEWBY. Yes, sir. Yes, sir. (*The four of them go.*)

MRS. HUFFMASTER. That horse is going to kick you in the head. . . . Whose is he?

MARY. My husband got him for the heavy work.

MRS. HUFFMASTER. (*Sits, takes off her shoes, rubs bare and dirty feet.*) What a relief to get off my feet after working on the patch. . . . What heavy work? Your menfolk seem to be getting in the way of each other doing nothing at all. . . . If that horse gives you a kick in the head, I'll give him a piece of sugar for a reward.

MARY. My husband hired him cheap.

MRS. HUFFMASTER. Mrs. Smith, could you give me a drink of water—with that raspberry syrup. The same like you gave me yesterday. . . . All day long you knit the same gray scarf. But it's not the same scarf. I see you begin one and knit your way through until it's finished—and then you begin a new one. What do you need them all for with only a father and two brothers?

MARTHA. I have other menfolk at home.

MARY. (*Interrupts, cutting off the discussion.*) I'm sure this will refresh you, Mrs. Huffmaster.

MRS. HUFFMASTER. (*Indicating the kerchief around Mary's throat.*) I never see any work done at all on this farm. . . . That's very pretty. It would look nice on me, Mrs. Smith.

MARY. Would you like to try it on, Mrs. Huffmaster?

MRS. HUFFMASTER. Now that you've asked. (*She tries it on.*) If that horse spills your brains out, I won't even bother to pick them up. . . . It becomes me, doesn't it, Mrs. Smith?

MARY. Keep it, Mrs. Huffmaster. I have another.

MRS. HUFFMASTER. Do you know, Mrs. Smith, people are gossiping about this farm.

MARY. What about, Mrs. Huffmaster?

MRS. HUFFMASTER. They are farmers, but they don't farm. (*She points to a cloth on the table.*) Now that's what I call a lovely tablecloth. I have just the table for it. . . . I heard that a patrol might make you a visit to see what's going on. The officer in charge of the patrol came to me, seeing as I have my patch so close, and I told him—Have you maybe five pounds of flour until my cash comes in? . . . And I told them how you were just ready to get started. . . . And a little sugar while you're at it . . . Yes, that's what I told them. . . . Let that cat's tail alone. (*Mary brings her the items.*) Thank you, Mrs. Smith, you're a good neighbor. . . . Don't pull up geranium plants. Go pick weeds. (*She starts off.*) I'll come back in the afternoon and drink some more of your cold raspberry juice—that is, if I'm invited. . . . If you hurt any of those chickens, I'm going to bite you until I draw blood. (*She is off.*)

MARTHA. What does she know?

MARY. We can keep her quiet by stuffing her with gifts and food.

MARTHA. For how long?

MARY. I'll give her the tablecloth the next time. (*Calling up to the attic.*) She's gone. (*The men come down from the attic. They resume their activities in absolute silence. Cards are dealt; checker boards are set up; some of the men read; one man whittles with anger; Tidd irons in quiet fury.*)

TAYLOR. (*Notebook in hand and pencil poised, to Leeman who is reading a magazine.*) Please read aloud.

LEEMAN. (*Reads romantically as Taylor takes it down in his notebook.*) "As they walked toward the water's edge he took her dainty hand in his. He turned to her and said, 'Is there hope for me?' "

TIDD. (*Breaking in, to Taylor.*) For three nights in succession you've dreamed you're going to be killed when we attack?

TAYLOR. Yes.

TIDD. You believe in your dreams?

TAYLOR. I shall be killed at Harpers Ferry.

TIDD. Then why are you continually improving your mind? One hour of history, an hour of mathematics, an hour of shorthand—every day.

TAYLOR. For the same reason that you learn to bake, sew, knit, iron those shirts.

TIDD. I do these things in order to pass time away, so as not to perish from boredom. My object is only to get through each day safely. Each day unto itself. But you are improving your mind for the future. What future, since you are going to be cut down at Harpers Ferry?

TAYLOR. What would I do with the years of my life were I to live the Biblical three score and ten? Would I spend them in idleness, waiting for death to enfold me? I would improve myself to my fullest capacities. And that is exactly what I am now doing—and shall continue to do whether the allotted span of my life is measured in years or days. (*To Leeman.*) Please go on. (*John Brown, Newby, Oliver and Owen come in.*)

TIDD. Captain, this is your shirt. It gives me pleasure to burn a hole through it. (*Mary tries to take the iron away. He doesn't let her. Then he goes to where Osborn Anderson and Thompson are playing checkers, flips the board, scattering the checkers.*) Let us get on with Harpers Ferry.

JOHN BROWN. We must wait.

TIDD. How much longer can we remain here without being discovered?

JOHN BROWN. It is a risk, but we must take it. We will wait.

TIDD. We have one advantage, surprise. Let us not dissipate it by delaying in this farmhouse.

NEWBY. He is right.

LEARY. I agree.

MARTHA. Lower your voices. You can be heard on the road.

TIDD. (*In a lower voice.*) I will shout if I feel like it. I pray you, get word to Harriet Tubman at once to come with her fifty men. And let us make a final gathering of whatever men are waiting in the East and in Kansas. Let us move, quickly.

NEWBY. Send word to Harriet Tubman.

OWEN. Yes.

JOHN BROWN. We cannot stir from this house. We will wait.

TIDD. We will wait. We will wait. Answer my argument. Prove me wrong. But don't just repeat "We will wait."

JOHN BROWN. We cannot attack Harpers Ferry. We must wait. (*In a rage, Tidd grabs the rifle out of John Brown's hands and hurls it to the floor.*)

TIDD. You are no longer my captain. (*This acts as a release upon some of the other men.*)

NEWBY. Nor mine.

OWEN. If you don't set a date for the attack, you are not my captain.

JOHN BROWN. You have said it. I am no longer your captain.

KAGI. He spoke in haste.

JOHN BROWN. Choose a new captain.

LEARY. New captain? How choose a new captain?

JOHN BROWN. By election. Mary, get paper and pencil.

LEEMAN. It is the waiting.

KAGI. Captain, don't let the hard argument of a bitter day jeopardize our cause.

JOHN BROWN. Do you think this is the bitterness of a bitter day? I am calling for this vote, because it is the only way to hold our Army together. . . . Vote! Choose a captain. (*Mary has distributed paper and pencil. She takes a cap and goes around collecting the ballots in it during the following.*)

TIDD. Let me make my position clear. I am for John Brown, but I am not for Harpers Ferry. I do not believe in Harpers Ferry. It is a trap.

MARY. (*Interjects, overriding Tidd.*) He who believes in John Brown must believe in Harpers Ferry. The two are one.

TIDD. Most of us will be marching to our death when we go down into Harpers Ferry. But when this Army marches, my conscience has committed me to march with it. Because a blow must be struck. Because a bell must be sounded to awaken all. We are the bell and the tongue of the bell and the ringer of the bell, all in one. But the raid will fail and most of us will be killed. So why are we endangering that one small element we have in our favor—surprise?

MARY. (*Stands before Tidd, the last man to cast his ballot.*) Vote! You above all people in this house must vote! (*Tidd studies the men; then in angry despair, writes on his slip and drops it into the cap. Mary gives cap to Owen.*)

OWEN. (*To Tidd.*) Make the tally with me. (*There is silence as Owen and Tidd count the ballots.*)

TIDD. (*Picks up the rifle and hands it to John Brown.*) You are our Captain.

MARY. And you? How have you voted?

TIDD. (*Turning from her, to John Brown.*) I too have voted for you. All of us, without exception, have voted for you. . . . How far apart you and I are in our estimate of the success of our attack on Harpers Ferry—yet how united we are as to its necessity.

MARTHA. Attention. Attention. A man has turned in at the gate.

KAGI. Are we to have no peace today? (*The men start toward the attic, picking up all evidence of their presence.*)

MARTHA. It's John Cook. (*John Cook enters. He is 29 years old. There are quick greetings. John Brown, Kagi and Stevens take Cook aside. The general lighting dims as the lights come up more brightly on their area. All the other characters freeze.*)
COOK. I have only a few minutes. (*He unfolds a map and indicates on it as necessary.*) Here is a detailed map of Harpers Ferry showing buildings, the Armory, the Arsenal, streets and alleys. Here I show how the heights across the Shenandoah River merge into the Allegheny Mountains. A quick march and we are in the mountain wilderness. Exactly the way you said it would be when you sent me down here a year ago to study the land.
JOHN BROWN. You have performed your task well.
COOK. (*With self-satisfaction.*) During the day, I work as lock tender on the canal. In my spare time, I peddle books—Bibles, "The Life of George Washington," and maps. But this map—I have been working on it for a year. Gradually filling it in.
KAGI. All this accomplished—and he still has had time to find a pretty girl, court and marry her.
COOK. This heavily marked large farm belongs to Col. Lewis Washington, the great-grandnephew of George Washington. Until last week I could find no natural excuse to visit him. Then it occurred to me I should try to sell him a copy of "The Life of George Washington, Father of Our Country."
KAGI. A logical customer for such a book.
COOK. He bought four copies—one for himself, the other three for relatives. Even invited me for a glass of sherry. Even showed me the sword which General Lafayette had presented to George Washington. I held it in my hand.
JOHN BROWN. What sword did you say?
COOK. The sword which George Washingston received from Lafayette. It is an exquisite sword.
JOHN BROWN. It is more than a sword. When we strike Harpers Ferry, I will send a detachment to call on Col. Washington. I must have that sword. The slave will see the sword that George Washing-

ton held in his hand, which helped to free the white man and now helps to free the black.

COOK. Can I be part of that detachment? (*John Brown nods. Cook laughs.*) He's going to be surprised to see me. . . . I must go now.

JOHN BROWN. Will you stay for supper?

COOK. I've overstayed my time. My wife doesn't know where I am. I must return as quickly as possible. (*He begins to move off, then turns back. Impulsively.*) Captain, my wife is very young and has had no experience in life. She thinks I am what I appear to be—a lock tender on the canal who peddles books on the side, with a passion for roaming the countryside making maps. At night in bed, when all is quiet and she reaches out her hand to hold mine for a moment just before falling asleep, my soul cries out to tell her the truth.

JOHN BROWN. This is the lot of every conspirator. The more worthy the person, the greater his pain. And we are conspirators.

COOK. I know if I tell her the truth, she will be converted to our cause.

JOHN BROWN. (*Coldly.*) The risk is too great. You will continue to be as dumb as death to her.

COOK. Yes, Captain. (*He goes. The lights dim to black on this area. John Brown, Kagi and Stevens join the others and freeze with them. The lights remain dim on the "freeze" area and come up on Martha and Oliver in the orchard.*)

MARTHA. The men know that we have gone off together.

OLIVER. I am afraid they do. . . . Black clouds are piling up. Look at that thundercloud.

MARTHA. The world knows a wife and husband have pleasure in each other's bodies—but it does not know the exact intimate moment. But they in that house—they know the hour, almost the minute. When we are together, I sometimes feel as though a third person were present, brushing past, touching my skin.

OLIVER. Has anyone in there ever made you feel embarrassed, uncomfortable, when we go off, given you any sign, a smile, a glance?

MARTHA. No, not from a single one of them. But still it is there; the third person, the brushing past, the touching of my skin.

OLIVER. I am sorry you feel this.

MARTHA. Oliver, husband, kiss me. (*They kiss.*) I have enjoyed being with you in the open field when we were back home. But here, where we have only the open field, I long to be with you in a bed.

OLIVER. What will history say about our story?

MARTHA. How conscious you are of history. Everyone in this farmhouse—so conscious of history.

OLIVER. And so are you, my dear. . . . If we succeed, the world will call us heroes and a flag will fly over this house.

MARTHA. And if you fail?

OLIVER. If we fail? Most of us will be killed and the survivors will hang between heaven and earth.

MARTHA. (*Kisses him.*) Dear husband, I am with child.

OLIVER. This child of ours, conceived on slave soil, will live to see this very piece of earth become free soil for free men. I swear it, Martha, I swear my life on it. . . . The wind is stirring.

MARTHA. Leaves are trembling.

OLIVER. The air is turning cool.

MARTHA. Black clouds.

OLIVER. It is raining on the other side of the mountains. It will be with us in a minute.

MARTHA. The first drops. Hurry. Run.

OLIVER. Run. (*As they race into the house, the lights dim on orchard area and come up on area of house. It is a violent storm, with heavy thunder. The group breaks the "freeze".*)

KAGI. (*In a very loud voice.*) Listen everybody. We can shout. Make noise. The storm will drown out our sound. Make all the noise you can. The thunder is our cover. (*To the accompaniment of heavy thunder and lashing rain, the following takes place: general shouting; high-pitched screams; a jigging accompanied by pig-like squeals; crowing rooster; other animal sounds; whistling; four men carry out a wild drill—"To the left, march. To the right, march.*

About face. Company halt." One man takes a tin cup and plate and bangs madly; a few men pair off and wrestle; one man quietly begins to sing "Lorena" (music at end of play). First one, then another, and gradually others join the song. Soon all of the men are singing. The storm begins to abate.) Lower your voices. The storm is passing. (*The voices are lowered.*) Let there be quiet. (*Absolute silence. The men eye each other keenly.*)

TIDD. Let us go to bed. (*Mary lights four candles and hands them to the men. These men are interspersed in the line going up, so that every third or fourth man has a candle. The line goes up in silence as though part of a religious rite. There is complete silence.*)

OLIVER. (*Who is last on the line.*) Good night, Martha. Sleep well. Angels guard thee.

MARTHA. Good night. (*John Brown beckons to Kagi and Stevens. They join him in a partially darkened area downstage. They freeze during the following.*)

MARY. (*Holding up a shirt.*) Here's the shirt Tidd burnt.

MARTHA. (*Looks at it.*) It *isn't* Father's! He burned his own shirt. He was angry to the point of torment, but he would not injure another man's property.

MARY. Tomorrow I am going to teach him how to make a patch.

MARTHA. That will occupy him for half a day.

MARY. Let us go to bed, Martha, it is the end of the day. (*She looks in the direction of John Brown; softly.*) Good night, my dear and troubled husband. Good night. (*As Mary and Martha move off, the lights in their area dim and come up on John Brown, Kagi and Stevens. The three men unfreeze.*)

STEVENS. Well, we have gotten through this day safely.

KAGI. But can you guarantee another? Captain, why didn't you answer Tidd's argument with reason instead of repeating, "We will wait"? You forced the vote. Why?

STEVENS. Either we strike quickly as an army, a coordinated blow—

KAGI. Or each man will fly off by himself. Let us get a message at once to Harriet Tubman to come down from Canada with her fifty men, and let us— (*John Brown takes out a letter and shows it to Kagi. Kagi reads it rapidly and passes it on to Stevens.*) Dreadful. Dreadful news.

JOHN BROWN. That's why I forced the vote. (*Crying it out in grief.*) Harriet Tubman is sick in her bed. The many trips she has made into the South, gathering slaves, hiding in the swamps, forced marches, have—

KAGI. She has never even gotten to Canada.

JOHN BROWN. There are no fifty men waiting for us north of the border. We are alone.

STEVENS. But the men from Kansas and the East.

JOHN BROWN. (*Bitterly, as he takes several letters from his pocket.*) I had a superb collection of letters this morning. (*Holding up a letter.*) Henry Carpenter will not join us. He started down, lost heart, and turned back. (*Holds up another.*) Luke Parsons has defected. George Gill, defected. Alexis Hinkley held himself in readiness for a year; now he cannot join us because of family troubles. . . . The whole family of man is troubled! . . . Oh, a few more men will come in—but I doubt we'll total thirty. My plan called for one hundred men.

STEVENS. Must we disband and come together at a better time?

JOHN BROWN. I have prepared myself for twenty years. Every turn and bend and twist of my life has been moving, step by step, towards this goal. I am 59 years old. Now is that moment, thrusting my life into the fire if need be, pitting my life against the life of slavery. I will not give up. We have lost fifty men from Canada.

KAGI. *And* Harriet Tubman.

JOHN BROWN. A blow, but not decisive. What is needed is something to replace the value of those fifty men.

KAGI. *And* Harriet Tubman.

JOHN BROWN. We must find a man—one single man. He must be an escaped slave, a man of judgment and bravery, a powerful orator. A Negro whose heroic deeds are known even to the most benighted slave in the darkest corner of slavery. I cannot go to the slaves—I am a prisoner of my white skin. But this Negro—when he says to the slave, "Rise up, take this weapon," there will be no hesitation.

KAGI. Frederick Douglass!

STEVENS. Douglass—yes!

JOHN BROWN. Frederick Douglass.

KAGI. You do not have the right even to ask him to join us. His newspaper reaches thousands of people.

JOHN BROWN. Is the editing of an anti-slavery paper more important than the firing of a rifle and the freeing of an army of slaves? He will have to suspend his work for a short period of time.

KAGI. Frederick Douglass' life is too valuable to risk in this venture.

JOHN BROWN. Are you saying our lives are less valuable than his?

KAGI. Yes! Our lives are less valuable than his.

JOHN BROWN. (*Brushing aside their objections.*) In the final balance, our lives will be measured by what we accomplish. I am asking him to meet me in secret near the abandoned quarry outside of Chambersburg. Kagi, you will go with me. I know Frederick Douglass will join us. (*The lights fade on this area and come up on the playing area of the abandoned quarry near Chambersburg. The quarry, filled with water, has become a pool. John Brown and Kagi move into the quarry area as Frederick Douglass and Shields Green come in from the other side. Douglass is a Mulatto, Green is a full-blooded Negro. John Brown and Douglass occupy center of area. Kagi and Green are out of the major focus of scene until indicated, watching the two principals intently. There is scarcely any pause between John Brown's last speech and the following.*) A year ago I could talk about Harpers Ferry only in general terms. But now with the information gathered by Cook, I am positive the attack can succeed.

DOUGLASS. Nothing you have said has changed my mind. Harpers Ferry is a steel trap. One jaw of the trap is the bridge over the Potomac River, the other jaw is the bridge over the Shenandoah.

JOHN BROWN. Listen to me. Listen to me. At the Potomac Bridge there is only one watchman. We overpower him and enter Harpers Ferry. Then a few of our men will capture the Arsenal and the Armory— (*Holds up a restraining hand as Douglass attempts to interject.*) It sounds more grand than it is; there is but a single watchman at the Armory gate. I will have control of Harpers Ferry for thirty hours, during which time the slaves will rise up in numbers and join our banner. These are the hours, Frederick, when God and I have crucial need for you.

DOUGLASS. Soft, soft, my friend. We haven't yet come to the moment of my participation.

JOHN BROWN. Before the town is able to organize a defense, we will march across the Shenandoah Bridge and then set fire to it. And the host will be covenanted on the other side of the burning bridge—the bridge behind us, the mountain range before us. (*Again he holds up his hand to forestall Douglass.*) A short, hard climb of several miles and we are safe in the mountain ranges—safe in the Alleghenies.

DOUGLASS. Again, you are already up in the mountains.

JOHN BROWN. Once there, no force can dislodge us. Two dozen men can hold back a thousand. We will swoop down on the flat plateau lands, gather up our slaves and retreat back into the mountains. (*Douglass impatiently tries to interrupt. John Brown holds up a hand to cut him off.*) It is an Army I am talking about, an Army in continuous operation recruiting its further soldiers from the ranks of the slaves it has liberated. (*Douglass tries to interrupt; again John Brown pushes on.*) We will destroy the money value of slave property—for no master will know when a piece of his human property worth fifteen hundred dollars will disappear in the night to join us in the mountains. I begin at the outside rim of the slave states, Virginia; as I push deeper, I force a continual shrinking up of the slave area. . . . All this is possible to attain. Is it not worth a great risk?

DOUGLASS. (*Quiet and deliberate.*) How many men have you at the present moment?

JOHN BROWN. At this moment my Army consists of seventeen men.
DOUGLASS. And how many more men can you expect by the night of the attack?
JOHN BROWN. Perhaps ten—perhaps five.
DOUGLASS. So—your maximum force will be about twenty-five men? And with this band you plan to—
JOHN BROWN. Army—not band.
DOUGLASS. And with this band you—
JOHN BROWN. Army. Not band. We are a legal body with a military organization.
DOUGLASS. Call it "Army" if you insist. But the enemy you fight will consider you nothing more than a rebel band.
JOHN BROWN. Not so many years ago my grandfather, Captain John Brown, by name, as I am named, fought against King George and the English. They who fought in the Revolutionary War were also called rebels. But it is victory or defeat which determines whether they be heroes or traitors. I expect finally to win this great campaign, therefore call it "Army"—an Army in the mountain wilderness.
DOUGLASS. Again you are in that mountain wilderness! But I see you trapped in Harpers Ferry. The raid will fail. There will be no army in the mountains. There will only be the desolate fact of twenty-odd men carrying out a doomed raid on a Southern town, trapped, captured, tried, found guilty, hanged.
JOHN BROWN. What are you saying to me, Frederick Douglass?
DOUGLASS. I am pleading with you not to go on this raid. I am saying to you further, if you insist on going, I will not join you.
JOHN BROWN. Frederick—Frederick—do not say this to me. (*Two rifle shots are heard in rapid succession. John Brown and Kagi seize their rifles. Douglass and Green take out their revolvers. All stand motionless. The following speeches are whispered.*)
KAGI. Slave catchers. (*Kagi listens intently.*) One set of footsteps. One man.
DOUGLASS. Into the underbrush. (*He motions to Green. They go quickly.*)

JOHN BROWN. (*Sits at edge of pool, rifle by his side. Gets his fishing rod, a sturdy six-foot pole from edge of pool, takes a worm from a packet and baits his hook. To Kagi.*) Sit there. Read your book. Have your rifle ready.

KAGI. (*Does so.*) Why bother with a worm?

JOHN BROWN. It would offend my sense of completion if the worm were omitted. . . . Do I look like a farmer spending a quiet hour?

KAGI. Exactly. But, please, don't flick your wrist so energetically. There are no fish in the quarry. (*A deer-hunter with a rifle enters rapidly. He is surprised to stumble on them.*)

THE DEER-HUNTER. Hello! I had no idea—

JOHN BROWN. I give you the blessings of the day, young man.

THE DEER-HUNTER. Thank you, old farmer. I am trailing a deer which I just shot. Did you hear any plunging in the thicket?

KAGI. (*Rising, looks off.*) There! We heard something over there.

THE DEER-HUNTER. (*Starts off, then turns and looks at John Brown intently.*) Any fish in that quarry?

JOHN BROWN. First time we've been here. (*The deer-hunter goes. John Brown continues fishing. Kagi looks after the deer-hunter, indicates that all is safe. Douglas and Green return.*)

DOUGLASS. (*Studies John Brown in silence for a moment before beginning.*) It is your thought that the slaves will rise up and flock to your banner if you have a strong, persuasive Negro voice to assure them it's no betrayal?

JOHN BROWN. That is so.

DOUGLASS. And you plan to incorporate these newly arisen slaves into your Army?

JOHN BROWN. Yes.

DOUGLASS. You are in error. The Canadians are the bravest and most experienced of my people. To escape, a slave had to dare bullet and bloodhound, swamp and mountain. Many failed. In Canada, they have been trained in the uses of the rifle and the pistol. Yes. The Canadians could have been incorporated into your Army in a single day. Not so the slaves from this area. Some will make capable soldiers; others will not. (*John Brown makes as if to interject. Douglass prevents him.*) Second, there is the question of training. It is a crime punishable by death for a slave to *hold* a rifle in his hand. It will take weeks, months, before they can learn to shoot. Yet when you strike Harpers Ferry your Army must be ready. The one thing you do not have is the six months' time necessary to train your Army.

JOHN BROWN. (*Takes the sturdy six-foot fishing pole, and forcefully tears the line off it. Then he takes from his pocket a black steel object, which proves to be the blade of a pike. He fits blade onto shaft and holds it aloft.*) Here is my solution to that problem.

DOUGLASS. What is it?

JOHN BROWN. A pike.

DOUGLASS. A pike?

JOHN BROWN. For hundreds of years, in Europe, the pike has been the weapon of the foot soldier. Until they learn how to use a rifle, these newly freed soldiers will use the pike.

DOUGLASS. A pike!

JOHN BROWN. (*Thrusts blade hard at Douglass' body, stopping short an inch away from Douglass' chest.*) Would you like to be at the sharp end of this weapon with a determined man behind it? I have a thousand of them, the blades and the poles, waiting for a thousand slaves to rise up and take them in their hands.

DOUGLASS. A pike! The rifle has changed the techniques of warfare. Fighting is no longer hand-to-hand combat.

JOHN BROWN. I foresee much close-quarter fighting. Besides, the pikes are an in-between measure until each man learns the rifle. Go on to your next point.

DOUGLASS. But you haven't answered the original point, namely, that newly arisen slaves who have never held a rifle in their hands cannot be substituted for bold, strong, well-trained Canadians.

JOHN BROWN. Go on to your next point.

DOUGLASS. It is your expectation that a multitude of slaves will arise when they hear of your raid on Harpers Ferry?

JOHN BROWN. It is.

DOUGLASS. False. There is no heavy Negro population here. This is farming country—farming country. There are a few slaves on one farm, several on another. It is only in the deeper South, on the large plantations, that there are heavy concentrations of slaves—fifty—a hundred on a plantation. But not in Virginia. (*John Brown tries to interrupt. Douglass cuts him off.*) I give you the reality of the situation; accept it as such. . . . And why attack the Federal Government Armory and Arsenal? Surely you realize that by attacking the Federal Government, it has no choice but to crush you.

JOHN BROWN. God is with us. Who can prevail against us?

DOUGLASS. The Federal Government. Or, do you think it will stand by idly even though you have captured its buildings, seized its weapons, made prisoner its employees?

JOHN BROWN. I chose Harpers Ferry precisely because it has the Armory and the Arsenal. I am pitting my morality against that of the Government of the United States. It is both right and necessary for a man who believes that his government is committing a crime against God and against the least and the last and the lowliest of this land, to rise up and match his morality against that of his government. I believe in the ultimate goodness of the people of this land. Once we are in the mountains, my Army with its pikes will place this question of slavery squarely before them. They will be faced with it in their waking and their sleeping—and oh, the discomfort of squirming away from commitment—until one day squirming is no longer possible. When that time comes, the people will decide with me and with my Army. Is all this not worth a great risk?

DOUGLASS. My reason and my understanding tell me that you will fail, that Harpers Ferry will end in that final desolate fact of capture and death. But how I pray that I am wrong. If only I am wrong!

JOHN BROWN. Come with me, Frederick. I will defend you with my life.

DOUGLASS. I do not ask you to defend me with your life. I am ready to give my life when necessary. But I am not ready to throw

my life away. I have work to do and I have a responsibility toward it.
KAGI. Let me ask you a question. Would you join us in the raid if you thought it would be successful?
DOUGLASS. No. I still would not go. The tools to him who can use them. Raiding is not my work.
KAGI. But what if, by joining us, the scales will be turned, the weight and balance of the situation changed sufficiently to bring about success?
DOUGLASS. I have a responsibility to the work I do. To let myself be deflected would be doing a disservice to the cause for which we both do battle. . . . It would be easier for me to say, "Yes. I will go with you to Harpers Ferry." But "No" it is. I have a different path to travel.
JOHN BROWN. Then two men, both dedicated to the same cause, at the self-same moment, can take totally opposite courses of action and yet each be correct and justified?
DOUGLASS. (*Nods slowly and soberly.*) Totally opposite courses of action, yet each justified.
JOHN BROWN. Then—it is right for you not to go. Go back to Rochester and your paper. As for me—it is my task to strike at Harpers Ferry. My entire life has been shaping to this final expression of my love of God and the need to see all the children of the human family equal in freedom.
DOUGLASS. I plead with you, do not go—but I know you will. (*He clasps John Brown.*)
JOHN BROWN. You say goodbye to me as though for the last time.
DOUGLASS. It is. It is the last time. (*He turns and silently shakes hands with Kagi. Then he motions to Green to go.*)
GREEN. (*To John Brown.*) Will it do good, the raid, even if it fails?
JOHN BROWN. If we win, we will win greatly. But even if we fail at Harpers Ferry, we will still win. (*Green turns to Douglass for confirmation.*)
DOUGLASS. It will do good.

GREEN. Even if it fails?
DOUGLASS. Even if it fails.
GREEN. I go then with the old man. (*John Brown puts his rifle in Green's hands. John Brown and Douglass turn away from each other and go off a few steps in opposite directions. Then suddenly and rapidly, they turn back and go into each other's arms, clasping one another. They kiss the other's cheek. There is a quick moment of silent grief. Douglass starts off. John Brown calls out after him.*)
JOHN BROWN. Go your way, Frederick Douglass, go your way. My way is to Harpers Ferry. (*The lights fade on this area and come up on the area of the Kennedy Farmhouse as John Brown, Kagi and Green move into the Farmhouse area. All the men are present in the Farmhouse including Cook; they are armed. Each man wears a long gray scarf around his neck. They are the scarves which Martha has been knitting. Mary and Martha are not present. There is scarcely any pause between John Brown's last speech and this one.*) Men, take up your arms. We march down on Harpers Ferry.
KAGI. Attention! Form a column of twos. (*The men form in twos.*) Gentlemen, the Commander-in-Chief of the Provisional Army—Captain John Brown.
JOHN BROWN. From the Table of Organization, you know each company in our Army consists of 72 soldiers. (*With an edge of irony and wit.*) But some of you who have been appointed captains do not have a single soldier under your command for the reason that at this moment your company consists of yourself alone. (*Most serious.*) But our Army will grow. And who will be able to stand up against our Army in the mountains? . . . Take out your maps. (*Each of the men takes a map from his pocket.*) We move on Harpers Ferry two at a time. Captains Tidd and Cook, you two will lead the Army, fifty yards ahead of the column. If you meet anyone, detain him in loud conversation, so the rest of the Army can get off the road and hide in the brush. When you get to the spot I have marked on your maps, cut the telegraph wires. (*To all.*) The moment the wires are cut, the plan goes into operation. You all have your

instructions. Follow them without fail. (*There is a short pause. Gravely.*) Captain Watson Brown and Private Taylor, your task is especially important. As quickly as you can after we enter Harpers Ferry, take control of the bridge over the Shenandoah River. Keep control of it. At all costs, keep control. It is our path into the mountains. (*Giving a carpetbag to Owen.*) Captain Owen Brown, you and Private Barclay Coppoc are to remain here on guard. Tomorrow morning I will send wagon and men to load our belongings. The instant the house is cleared, join us at Harpers Ferry. Be sure this bag goes with you. It contains my papers and documents. (*To all.*) Remember and remember again—no noise. If a man resists, use knife or sword. No shot is to be fired except in extreme emergency. Knife or sword, but no bullet. (*After a brief silence, John Brown raises his free hand in benediction.*) May the Angels of the Lord enfold and protect you. (*Pause. . . . then.*) Captain Kagi, arrange the line-up for the march.

KAGI. Soldiers, file outside.

JOHN BROWN. (*Only he and the two men who are the rear guard, remain. John Brown, rifle in the crook of his arm, stands erect.*) Lord, God of Justice and Wrath, I have heard the weeping in Egypt. I go to my work. (*He goes. From far off the roll of a drum is heard. The lights dim rapidly. Blackout.*)

END OF ACT ONE

Act II

Midnight. The Armory grounds. The Fire-Engine House is to one side; there is open ground on the other. John Brown, Kagi and a few of the men are present. Until indicated all dialogue is whispered.

COOK. (*Enters rapidly.*) We have cut the telegraph wires. Harpers Ferry is sealed off from the outside world. (*He goes off rapidly. Newby enters with a short-bladed sword poised at the back of a white prisoner whom he is driving before him. John Brown signals to one of the men who takes the prisoner into the Fire-Engine House.*)
JOHN BROWN. (*To Newby.*) The bridge over the Shenandoah?
NEWBY. It is ours. And we have two more prisoners. Assign another man to bring them back with me.
LEEMAN. (*Enters.*) We have taken possession of the Arsenal building.
JOHN BROWN. Good. Private Leeman, go with Private Newby and bring back the prisoners from the Shenandoah Bridge. Hurry. (*Newby and Leeman go.*)
LEARY. (*Enters with a prisoner.*) Captain Stevens, Private Copeland and I have seized the Rifle Works. Here is the watchman. (*John Brown signals and one of the men takes the prisoner into the Fire-Engine House.*) Captain Stevens asks for a reinforcement of three men.
JOHN BROWN. (*Expansively.*) He shall have his three men. We have control of the two bridges, the Armory, the Arsenal, the Rifle

Works. Not fire a bullet, not be fired upon; not kill a man, not lose one of our own. (*The church bell has begun to ring.*) And all this by midnight. The South is vulnerable. It took 25 men—I thought it would need a hundred. We can carry out every step of the plan.
KAGI. But the time is close; by six in the morning, Harpers Ferry will be an angry beehive.
JOHN BROWN. Now for the reinforcements at the Rifle Works. (*A shot is heard. From here on, there is no further whispering. In a loud voice.*) Find out what's happened. (*Leary goes.*)
KAGI. The first shot in the battle. Now the town will be alerted. Six hours too soon.
JOHN BROWN. The men at the Rifle Works will have to wait for reinforcements. (*Lights fade into darkness. The beat of drums is heard. Drums stop. Lights come back up on the same scene of the Armory grounds. It is now noon. As will be seen from the action, one part of this open ground is in the line of fire, the other part is protected.*)
KAGI. Noon already. It won't be dark for at least six hours.
JOHN BROWN. Then we must hold out for at least six hours. When it gets dark— (*Shouts warningly.*) Leeman, stand back out of the line of fire!
KAGI. There is a crossfire. Get further back. Wait there.
JOHN BROWN. The town is fighting back sooner than I expected.
NEWBY. (*Has been peering out.*) Look. There. No. There. A sharpshooter. On top of the water tower. He's the one that's pinning us down. Captain, I'm going to bring him down.
KAGI. I shoot better than you. I'm going after him.
NEWBY. To me that man is Jesse Jennings. He owns my wife and seven children. I won't miss. (*He runs, aims, shoots and races back.*) The next man won't be in such a sweat to climb up there. (*John Brown signals. Leeman runs across the open area.*)
LEEMAN. (*To John Brown.*) Captain Stevens requests six men at once. Either that or give him permission to evacute the Rifle Works.
JOHN BROWN. The wagon has not yet returned from the Kennedy

Farmhouse. When it does, Captain Stevens will have his reinforcements. Go. (*Leeman starts off.*)
KAGI. (*To Leeman.*) Stay. (*Leeman stops. Kagi draws John Brown aside.*) Captain, I want to offer a suggestion.
JOHN BROWN. (*Curtly.*) Offer. I do not stop you.
KAGI. Weigh it carefuly. Do not reject it off-hand.
JOHN BROWN. (*Peremptorily.*) Your suggestion?
KAGI. Everything went perfectly for the first few hours. But now the town is fighting back with fury. We have lost the initiative. Furthermore, there has been no slave uprising. Sixteen in total.
JOHN BROWN. How could you expect them to come forward in the middle of the day? They would be shot down. As soon as night falls, they will come in twos and threes. All night, as word spreads over the countryside. . . . Your suggestion. What is it?
KAGI. Tell Stevens to withdraw.
JOHN BROWN. Abandon the Rifle Works?
KAGI. Abandon the Rifle Works. Draw in the men guarding the Arsenal. Get word to the men holding the Potomac Bridge to withdraw and join us. Gather our Army. Get across the Shenandoah Bridge. Set fire to it and then into the mountain wilderness.
JOHN BROWN. And the men at the Kennedy Farmhouse?
KAGI. We cannot risk the entire plan because—
JOHN BROWN. And the equipment at the Kennedy Farmhouse—military documents?
KAGI. If we retreat now we will have proved that a small band can attack a bastion of the South and take control of it. If we don't retreat now, we risk complete loss.
JOHN BROWN. (*Turns from Kagi, goes to Leeman.*) Tell Stevens to stand firm for one hour. (*Leeman runs across the open area and leaves. John Brown goes back to Kagi.*) We must gather fifty to one hundred slaves during the coming night.
KAGI. They will rise quickly in the deep South—not here in the border area. Remember the warning of Frederick Douglass.
JOHN BROWN. (*Suddenly changing tone, entreating.*) Give me

one hour. The men must return from the Kennedy Farmhouse within the hour.

KAGI. It will be a costly hour. (*He moves away.*)

COL. WASHINGTON. (*Coming from rear where he and the other prisoners are stationed. He is faultlessly dressed.*) Captain Brown?

JOHN BROWN. What is it, Col. Washington?

COL. WASHINGTON. (*Indicating belt of sword.*) May I adjust the belt for you? You will be more comfortable.

JOHN BROWN. Thank you.

COL. WASHINGTON. (*As he adjusts the belt.*) I see very few men about me. Where are the bulk of your troops?

JOHN BROWN. You forget. *I* do the questioning.

COL. WASHINGTON. If your troops are in the hills of Maryland, why don't they come over the Potomac Bridge since you control it? If they are up in the Heights, why don't they come down since you control the Shenandoah Bridge? As a military man, I am puzzled.

JOHN BROWN. You will learn what you have to learn when I am ready for you to know it. . . . Are you through, sir? I have no further time for you.

COL. WASHINGTON. That should be more comfortable.

JOHN BROWN. So it is. (*Sardonically.*) That is very courteous, Col. Washington. Especially since it was yours less than ten hours ago.

COL. WASHINGTON. (*Answering him in kind.*) Take care of it, sir. It will be mine again before long. (*A shouting and cheering is heard from afar.*)

JOHN BROWN. Kagi! Kagi! Our men are coming from the farmhouse!

KAGI. Why would townspeople cheer the arrival of our wagon? (*He looks out.*) Soldiers are rushing to the bridge.

JOHN BROWN. (*To Col. Washington.*) Are you familiar with the soldiery of this area?

COL. WASHINGTON. I am the military aide to the Governor of Virginia. (*John Brown points toward the men approaching the bridge.*) The Jefferson Volunteer Guards from Charles Town.

JOHN BROWN. They could not have been marched here so quickly.
COL. WASHINGTON. Unless my eyes deceive me, they are here. Did you think they were your men? Where are your men, Captain? I count two holding the bridge and rapidly approaching are at least a hundred men well armed. Far be it from me to advise you, Capt. Brown, but I suggest that you reinforce your guard on the bridge with at least twenty men—preferably thirty. And at once.
JOHN BROWN. Hold your tongue, sir. Withdraw to the other prisoners. (*Col. Washington bows sardonically and moves to the rear. John Brown barks out the orders to Kagi.*) Take two men to cover the retreat from the Potomac Bridge. Get our men from the Armory yard. Tell the men in the Arsenal to give up the building. Tell Stevens to retreat from the Rifle Works and join us. We will cover you with rifle fire.
NEWBY. I want to go.
KAGI. (*Nods assent. He calls out.*) Anderson. (*Jeremiah Anderson comes to his side.*) Come. (*Kagi, Newby and Jeremiah Anderson go off quickly as Leeman runs in panting and rushes to John Brown. Leeman has a wound in his upper left arm; his shirt sleeve is bloodstained.*)
LEEMAN. Look, Captain, look. I'm shot in the arm. A few inches more and it would have been my heart. I would have been dead, Captain.
JOHN BROWN. (*Shakes him.*) Give me Stevens' message.
LEEMAN. Stevens? Stevens? (*Then recalling.*) Oh, Stevens. I couldn't get to him. My way was cut off. The Rifle Works is surrounded. I saw at least fifty men charge the building. There was a faint answering fire. But Stevens and his two men can't hold out for more than a few minutes.
JOHN BROWN. Bind your wound. Rest. (*Leeman goes as Watson and Taylor enter. Taylor has a scalp wound; one side of his face has a small trickle of blood.*) The bridge! The Shenandoah Bridge! Why aren't you at your posts? It's our gateway to the mountains.
WATSON. We were driven off by dozens of armed men.

JOHN BROWN. We will continue the fight from here.
TAYLOR. We are cut off. Shouldn't we surrender?
JOHN BROWN. There will be no surrender. (*Kagi, Jeremiah Anderson, Oliver and Thompson enter.*)
GREEN. Where's Newby? Where's Newby?
OLIVER. Buckshot tore his throat open from ear to ear. He's dead.
JOHN BROWN. And with his death goes the hope of his wife and seven children.
GREEN. (*Looks off.*) They are dragging his body near the wall.
KAGI. What are they doing to him?
COL. WASHINGTON. (*Who has been moving forward slowly.*) Cutting off his ears.
KAGI. Why?
COL. WASHINGTON. For souvenirs. We usually crop the ears of a runaway slave. This marks him as a malcontent.
JOHN BROWN. Rejoin the other prisoners. (*Col. Washington moves to rear.*) They're moving to surround us. Into the Fire-Engine House. We will consolidate our forces. (*They move into the Fire-Engine House.*)
OLIVER. There aren't any windows.
TAYLOR. If we fire from the doorway, we're a perfect target.
KAGI. Stand to the side of the door. Fire only when necessary.
OLIVER. (*Goes to doorway and kneels.*) Just this one shot. Watch me get that fellow with his eye over the wall. (*He aims, but he is hit by a bullet and falls to the ground. Taylor goes to his aid. He is hit and falls. John Brown helps Oliver away from door. Kagi carries Taylor from door.*)
KAGI. He is dead.
JOHN BROWN. (*Opens Oliver's coat and shirt and examines him. Oliver is in pain.*) I have no bandages, Oliver. Only this handkerchief. (*He bends over Oliver and works on him.*)
KAGI. (*Urgently to John Brown.*) Arrange for a parley. Now! Before the enemy realizes what a small force we have.
JOHN BROWN. (*To Oliver.*) I will be back in a minute. (*Leaves*

Oliver and points to a prisoner in the rear.) You. Prisoner, come forward.

PRISONER. Me? Why must it be me?

JOHN BROWN. Come forward. (*The prisoner advances.*) Captain Thompson, bring a pike. Go with this man and try to arrange a parley. Tell their commanding officer that your commanding officer is willing to arrange a cease-fire.

THOMPSON. Yes, Captain.

JOHN BROWN. (*Gives him a white handkerchief.*) Tie this to the pike.

KAGI. Wave your flag in a wide arc and very deliberately.

THOMPSON. (*To prisoner.*) Come along. (*With the prisoner before him, he steps out, waving the handkerchief on the pike. They cover a short distance, three men appear, seize Thompson and hustle him out of sight. The prisoner runs off.*)

JOHN BROWN. There must be a mistake. They didn't understand the purpose of the white flag.

COL. WASHINGTON. (*Moving forward into the scene.*) There was no mistake. They understood.

JOHN BROWN. Nobody would take prisoner a soldier bearing a flag of truce.

COL. WASHINGTON. Captain Brown, so far as Harpers Ferry is concerned, you are a band of desperadoes. I deplore taking prisoner a man carrying a white flag—but in this instance I understand it.

JOHN BROWN. It was the military that took possession of the bridge. It must be a mistake.

COL. WASHINGTON. By this time the town is filled with drunken people from all over the countryside. They will not obey military orders. And the Jefferson Guards—it is only a company of volunteers. It is no mistake.

KAGI. You heard him. Do you want to arrange for a parley without further loss of any of our men? Take the most important prisoner we've got. (*Points to Col. Washington.*) Him. Shoot him. Throw his body out of the door. Let ten minutes elapse for our action to sink in. Then send a Negro out with a white flag. (*John Brown makes a gesture of repugnance.*) They will not shoot a Negro; he is too valuable to them. Let them know we demand unmolested passage across the Shenandoah Bridge—that we are taking our prisoners as hostages to guarantee such passage and that we will release them unharmed on the other side of the bridge after we have set fire to it.

JOHN BROWN. Captain Kagi, Captain Watson Brown. Carry the flag of truce to the commanding officer of the Jefferson Volunteer Guards to arrange a cease-fire so we can withdraw from the town.

COL. WASHINGTON. (*As Watson tears off shirt tail and puts it on the head of a pike.*) Captain Brown, do not send these two men out. I do not want it said that Virginians shot at men carrying a flag of truce. And it will be said—for they will shoot.

JOHN BROWN. A parley is necessary. They will go. (*A prisoner comes forward and says.*)

ANDREW KITZMILLER. I'm Andrew Kitzmiller, Superintendent of the Armory. Everyone knows me. Let me go with them. No one will shoot if I shield them.

JOHN BROWN. I accept your honorable offer.

KITZMILLER. (*To Kagi and Watson.*) Stand close. Lock arms. One of you on either side. Close as you can get.

COL. WASHINGTON. (*To John Brown.*) These men shoot the heads off wild turkey on the wing so as not to pepper the meat with buckshot. Do you think there will be a problem picking off a man at fifty paces? (*To Kitzmiller.*) They will drop them on either side of you—drunk as they are.

OLIVER. (*Calling out.*) Don't send Watson. I am already wounded. We have given our fair share.

JOHN BROWN. (*To Oliver.*) Fair share? How do you measure fair share? In pounds and ounces, or yards and feet? Shall I send out another, hesitating to send my own son? (*To Watson.*) Wave the flag slowly from side to side.

WATSON. We are going to our death, Father.

JOHN BROWN. That may be, Captain Brown.

KITZMILLER. Stand close. Move slowly. Wave your flag broadly so there is no mistaking it. (*They go out, arms twined around each other's shoulders. Several shots are heard. Kitzmiller shouts.*) You all know me. Don't shoot. We are trying to arrange a truce. (*The firing ceases.*) Stay close to me. As close as you can get. (*They move about five paces with Watson waving the flag. Rifle shots. Kagi is hit. Kitzmiller tries to hold him up but Kagi goes down. More rifle shots and Watson sinks to the ground, the flag of truce clattering by his side. Kitzmiller shouts in rage and shame.*) Cowards. Cowards. Cowards. Cowards. Cowards. (*He slowly moves to the edge of the scene and is off. Col. Washington pushes John Brown aside, runs out and stands shielding Watson's body with his.*)

COL. WASHINGTON. (*Shouts.*) It is I, Col. Washington. Shoot me if you dare. (*Rifle fire stops. Watson crawls back into Fire-Engine House with Col. Washington closely following to shield him. As soon as Watson is in Fire-Engine House, Col. Washington says to John Brown.*) Take care of your son.

JOHN BROWN. He is a soldier in my Army.

COL. WASHINGTON. (*Points to Kagi.*) And your man, Kagi? He will bleed to death unless he is given medical attention. You cannot go after him. They will shoot. I will carry him off the field. The honor of Virginia has been sullied by the shooting of men carrying a flag of truce. I give you my word of honor that I will return as your prisoner directly I have put him in the hands of a doctor.

JOHN BROWN. May the Lord bless you on your errand.

COL. WASHINGTON. (*Goes out. A bullet is fired. He raises his arms and crosses them back and forth over his head.*) It is I, Col. Washington. (*There is no rifle fire. He goes to Kagi, picks him up and carries him off.*)

LEEMAN. Captain Brown, we'll be killed if we stay here. Let's try to escape. They're all watching Col. Washington. We can sneak out by the back way. If we run fast, we'll be able to reach the river.

JOHN BROWN. (*Grabs Leeman roughly by the jacket.*) Stay here, boy. (*In fury, he lifts him up from off the ground and then stamps him down hard.*) Don't move from this spot I'm planting you on. (*He turns his back squarely on Leeman and tends Watson's wounds. Then he goes to Oliver and tends his wounds. During this he calls out.*) Men, keep away from the door. (*Leeman looks furtively about, then darts out of Fire-Engine House. Instantly, firing is heard. Jeremiah Anderson peers out guardedly.*)

JEREMIAH ANDERSON. Captain, look!

JOHN BROWN. (*Leaves Oliver and looks out. Sadly.*) He is dead. He was only a boy. (*He goes back to tending Oliver.*)

JEREMIAH ANDERSON. They're using his body for target practice. (*Watches for a moment, fascinated and horrified, wincing as each bullet finds its mark on Leeman's body. He turns away, sees something and calls out.*) Col. Washington is coming back with another man. (*Then he turns away and begins sobbing.*)

COL. WASHINGTON. (*Enters with Dr. Starry. The front of Col. Washington's coat is stained red with blood. They go into Fire-Engine House.*) I have returned in accordance with my parole.

JOHN BROWN. I thank you for your virtue.

COL. WASHINGTON. You must pardon my appearance. I have no change of clothes. . . . The saloons are doing a rushing business. Everybody is drinking wildly, as though on a holiday—or on the edge of doom. Permit me to introduce you two gentlemen to each other. This is our host, Captain Brown; this is Dr. Starry. (*They acknowledge the introductions with a slight nod of the head.*) I carried your man Kagi to safety and Dr. Starry took care of him.

DR. STARRY. He is under military guard so that he won't be molested by drunken townspeople.

COL. WASHINGTON. Dr. Starry agreed to come here and dress the wounded.

DR. STARRY. (*To Oliver as he works on him.*) What brought you here?

OLIVER. Duty, sir.

DR. STARRY. Is it your idea of duty to shoot men down upon their hearthstones for defending their rights?

OLIVER. I did not come for pleasure—nor for my own interest. I am driven here by my duty. (*Dr. Starry finishes his work on Oliver and then tends to Watson. When he is finished, he goes to John Brown.*)

DR. STARRY. They are your sons? (*John Brown nods.*) I do not think either of them will survive.

JOHN BROWN. My men were shot down like dogs while bearing the flag of truce.

DR. STARRY. I am sorry for you as a father, but people making an insurrection must run the risk of being shot down like dogs. . . . I will come back before dark and fix them up for the night. Have you water?

JOHN BROWN. Almost none.

DR. STARRY. I will try to smuggle in a canteen for the wounded. (*He goes carrying his black medical bag in one hand, waving white handkerchief over his head with the other. The characters on stage freeze. The lights fade indicating a passage of time. The lights come up. The characters unfreeze. It is now shortly before dawn. There are to be appropriate light changes.*)

JOHN BROWN. (*Carries rifle throughout scene.*) Men, are you awake?

TWO VOICES. We are awake.

JOHN BROWN. Stay awake. It will soon be light. (*Goes to Oliver.*) How is it with you, my son?

OLIVER. Father, have mercy. Put me out of my pain. Shoot me.

JOHN BROWN. I will not shoot a soldier in my Army.

OLIVER. You would shoot a horse if he received a death-wound. Show the same mercy toward your son.

JOHN BROWN. No.

OLIVER. Is there any water?

JOHN BROWN. (*Gives him water.*) A cupful. (*As he goes to Watson, he calls out.*) There is not much time before dawn. Men, stay awake. (*He takes Watson's pulse.*) Watson?

WATSON. I am cold.

JOHN BROWN. Here is my scarf. (*Finds the sword getting in his way, unbuckles it impatiently and puts it down.*)

WATSON. Like a dog they shot me. Carrying a flag of truce.

JOHN BROWN. I saw it. And God saw it. Be comforted, my son. (*Gives him a drink of water, then begins tending him.*)

COL. WASHINGTON. (*Goes to John Brown. Col. Washington's objective is to undermine John Brown and get him to surrender. John Brown becomes increasingly irritated, wishing not to be disturbed as he takes care of Watson. He tries to cut off the exchange, but each time rises to the bait of Col. Washington's questions.*) Captain Brown, when I was captured and brought here in the early morning, you told me that you are God's partner whose appointed task it is to free the slaves.

JOHN BROWN. Yes.

COL. WASHINGTON. If you are God's partner, why are you failing?

JOHN BROWN. I have not yet failed.

COL. WASHINGTON. Oh, come, man. There are three—four thousand soldiers encircled around this building. The United States Marines have arrived from Washington. When daylight breaks, your doom is sealed. Why did God let you plunge into this hopeless fiasco?

JOHN BROWN. If Harpers Ferry is a failure, the fault is mine, mine alone.

COL. WASHINGTON. How so?

JOHN BROWN. God assigns the general task. It was I who selected Harpers Ferry.

COL. WASHINGTON. So. God is responsible for success and you for failure! That is most uneven-handed of Him. At what point in the course of an action, Captain, does the partner of God know fully the plans of God?

JOHN BROWN. He does not know them fully until the final moment of the action.

COL. WASHINGTON. You mean the plan is revealed to him hour by hour, minute by minute?
JOHN BROWN. How else?
COL. WASHINGTON. What if God's partner and spokesman misreads God's intention, misjudges? The action is a failure—as it had to be in view of the misreading of God's intention. Nay, further. What if God fashions a large design which calls for temporary defeat in order to achieve a greater ultimate good? And what if God's partner, not acquainted with the ultimate design, strives to avoid the temporary failure? Is he not at that moment acting against God's final design?
JOHN BROWN. (*Enraged with Col. Washington's insistent questioning, he leaves Watson and faces Washington with anger and contempt.*) Have I claimed that my relationship with God was that of Moses and the burning bush—that God talks to me and I with Him? Is this your understanding of what—
JEREMIAH ANDERSON (*At Oliver's side.*) Captain Brown.
JOHN BROWN. Oliver. Oliver. (*Rifle in hand, goes to Oliver and feels his pulse. He closes Oliver's eyes.*) He is dead.
GREEN. (*Has gone to attend to Watson while John Brown was with Oliver.*) Watson?
JOHN BROWN. (*Goes to Watson's side. He sees that Watson is dead. He closes Watson's eyes.*) This is my third son. Frederick, in Kansas—Watson—Oliver.
COL. WASHINGTON. (*Is not moved by these two deaths. He uses them in a further attempt to undermine John Brown.*) Do not stain your soul with further death. Open that door and surrender.
JOHN BROWN. Men, load and cock your rifles. Be sure you have plenty of ammunition by your side. (*The characters freeze as the lights dim down quickly and come up on another playing area showing Col. Robert E. Lee and Lt. J. E. B. Stuart.*)
COL. LEE. They're only a handful, Lt. Stuart. But they can drag out this disgraceful situation for many hours. There is only one way to dislodge them quickly. Cold steel at close quarters. Therefore,

Lieutenant, you will rush the Fire-Engine House. Then, the bayonet and sword.

LT. STUART. (*Salutes.*) Col. Lee, in the name of the United States Marines, I thank you for the honor. My men will enjoy finishing them off.

COL. LEE. You've never been in action before?

LT. STUART. No, sir.

COL. LEE. It is a minor skirmish. It will be over in three minutes.

LT. STUART. (*To Marines.*) Attention! Fix bayonets. (*The characters freeze. Lights fade and come up on playing area of Fire-Engine House. The characters in Fire-Engine House unfreeze.*)

COL. WASHINGTON. Captain Brown, if you are not totally mad, you must recognize by now that you are self-deceived in speaking for God. You have three men left. Count them. What can you possibly accomplish? Open that door and prevent further sacrifice of life.

JOHN BROWN. Stand aside. We have God's work to do. . . . Men, carry on the battle to the last breath.

COL. WASHINGTON. (*He has failed. He is raging.*) You are a madman.

JOHN BROWN. Certainly I am mad—as you view madness. I have gone mad over an idea—the idea that all men are equal. . . . Make every shot count. (*A platoon of Marines rush in. John Brown and his men fire at them as they enter. The first Marine falls dead; the second falls injured; the other Marines jump over the two fallen men and attack the four men of John Brown's army. Not more than 4 or 5 shots are fired by the defenders before they are overwhelmed. A Marine rushes toward Jeremiah Anderson, who cries out.*)

JEREMIAH ANDERSON. Surrender.

MARINE. (*Fiercely.*) Too late, sonny. (*He bayonets him.*)

COL. WASHINGTON. (*Calls out to Lt. Stuart as he points to John Brown.*) There's your man—the leader of the insurgents. (*Lt. Stuart rushes toward John Brown with sword extended. John Brown, who has been on one knee using his rifle, half-rises to fend off the ex-*

tended sword. He tries to use his rifle as a club, but Lt. Stuart sweeps it out of his hand and lunges at him, piercing him in the stomach. John Brown falls to the ground. Lt. Stuart raises his sword and strikes blows on John Brown's head. . . . The battle is over. Jeremiah Anderson lies dead; Edwin Coppoc and Green are prisoners; John Brown is on the floor.)

LT. STUART. (*Looks at his watch.*) Three minutes—almost to the second. Just as Col. Lee said. (*He opens John Brown's coat and looks down at him.*) He will be dead before the hour is out. (*To the Marines.*) Lay the dead and wounded out on the grass. As for him, carry him into the Paymaster's Room. (*Two Marines pick up John Brown.*)

COL. WASHINGTON. (*Takes the sword. To Lt. Stuart.*) This is my property. I will give accounting to your Commanding Officer. (*He extracts a pair of immaculate white kid gloves from his pocket and puts them on. Then, bowing sardonically to John Brown.*) I bid you good morning, Captain Brown. My stay with you has been most instructive. (*The lights dim as the two Marines deposit John Brown in the area of the Armory Paymaster's Room and move off. Simultaneously, Col. Washington moves into the next scene as the lights come up on another room in the Armory. Present are Gov. Henry A. Wise, Col. Lee, Lt. Stuart, Attorney Andrew Hunter, Sen. J. M. Mason of Virginia, Terence Byrne, a wealthy land and slave owner. They are examining maps and documents. From time to time, they take out further maps or documents from John Brown's overnight bag. Throughout the scene, Charles B. Harding, Attorney for Jefferson County, Virginia, is deep in drunken sleep; he snores occasionally. Two newspaper reporters stand in shadows off to one side, out of the focus of the scene.*)

HUNTER. And we don't know the full story. We know of over ten slaves who did get to him, and we already have reports of more than fifty who were stopped on the road and could give no reason for being there. How many would have gotten to him under cover of darkness if he had been able to hold out but one more night?

SEN. MASON. We must question every slave in the area. If he cannot give a scrupulous accounting of his whereabouts during the last forty-eight hours, he must be sold into the deep South. And we will crop his ears first, as a warning.

HUNTER. (*Bitterly.*) Sell our slaves into the deep South! For fifty years we have fought to extend slave territory. Now this one old man is forcing us to shrink up our slave area.

BYRNE. I propose, for the moral effect it will have, that we condemn one slave and hang him. And he must be valuable, to show that we are not trifling—that we are ready to destroy valuable property when necessary. All in favor say "Aye."

ALL. Aye.

SEN. MASON. Whose slave shall we hang? Which one?

BYRNE. My Ned is a superior piece of property. I would not like to lose him. But if necessary, I offer him for the hanging—especially since he disappeared for half the day.

COL. WASHINGTON. He could have been with his wife. Yesterday was Sunday, you know.

BYRNE. As far as I am concerned, the only place he could have been was on the way to the raiders.

SEN. MASON. What value do you place on him?

BYRNE. Twenty-five hundred dollars.

SEN. MASON. That's why he is ready to give up his Ned. He wants to make a profit on him.

BYRNE. He's worth every bit of twenty-five hundred dollars. I raised him from the time he was a boy. I treated him like my own child.

SEN. MASON. You all know my Henry. He is 23 years old, 180 pounds, good mouth, strong teeth, excellent wind, sound limbs. I measure my Henry up to your Ned, sir, in every respect, and I place a value on—

BYRNE. But my Ned is a skilled blacksmith.

SEN. MASON. And my Henry is a skilled carpenter. And I place a value on Henry of two thousand dollars. If you insist on holding out for twenty-five hundred, I'll offer my Henry in place of your Ned and we'll save five hundred.

BYRNE. Gentlemen, let us not haggle. Suppose we strike a figure of twenty-two fifty? Agreed? (*There are nods.*) I will expect your checks as soon as convenient.

HUNTER. I don't give a damn if Ned is hanged, or Henry—or both. This was not a slave uprising. It was an attack from the outside—from the North. The important thing is that old man, John Brown. What do we know about him? How large is his army? Where located? Is this the first contingent of an army of white Northerners? Will Virginia become the first battleground of a civil war? Has it come to this finally—civil war? These are the questions to which we must address ourselves—and at once. (*Lays out various maps.*) It all fits! Look at his plan! Look at these maps! White and slave population enumerated county by county for every state in the South. I will arrange these for you geographically. You will see a pattern emerge.

BYRNE. Fortunate for us that we found this bag of his.

COL. WASHINGTON. He did not intend to hold Harpers Ferry for a given period of time and then retreat back into Maryland. Harpers Ferry was but a stopping off point on his way to the mountains. He intended to take arms and ammunition from the Arsenal and then push into the mountain ranges of the South and carry on a guerrilla warfare.

HUNTER. Yes, you are right. Look at these maps. He could operate in the mountains, attack the lowlands, run off slaves, move up again into the mountains, always pressing deeper into the South.

COL. WASHINGTON. Here is his Provisional Constitution establishing a legal state—with a president, cabinet, organized army, articles of war, everything.

HUNTER. Let us go in immediately and interrogate that old man before he dies. Dr. Starry is with him now. (*They start toward the Paymaster's Room and freeze as the lights dim down and come up on the Paymaster's Room. John Brown lies on a pallet. Kagi lies near him on another pallet. Dr. Starry finishes tending John Brown.*)

DR. STARRY. Captain Brown, I have made you as comfortable as medicine knows how.

JOHN BROWN. I thank you, Dr. Starry. (*Dr. Starry leaves. John Brown and Kagi reach out their hands, but the pallets are a little too far apart. The outstratched fingertips do not quite touch. The hands fall, then are withdrawn.*)

JOHN BROWN. I have failed. I have betrayed God and Man.

KAGI. Don't be so hard on yourself.

JOHN BROWN. Do you have any news of my men?

KAGI. The Rifle Works was taken. Stevens and Leary are dead. Copeland has been captured.

JOHN BROWN. My sin is incalculable. There is no measure for it.

KAGI. My Captain, don't.

JOHN BROWN. And what happened to the other men?

KAGI. Thompson was dragged to the bridge by drunken townspeople, shot and thrown into the river. And Newby's body—I saw it all. About an hour after they cut his ears off, some men came and did a kind of war dance around him, jabbing his belly with sharp sticks. (*A counterpoint is to be established in the following speeches.*)

JOHN BROWN. Lord, God, why did You not let me die?

KAGI. The sticks ripped open his belly and his guts began to spill—

JOHN BROWN. Judas, my brother, I call to you across the ages.

KAGI. Then a pig came by and buried his snout in Newby's entrails—

JOHN BROWN. Judas, my brother, you betrayed God and Christ; I have betrayed God and Man.

KAGI. The pig took a ribbon of entrail in his mouth—

JOHN BROWN. Lord, God, my sin is mighty.

KAGI. The pig ran off dragging the entrail. A long ribbon between the pig's mouth and Newby's body. It grew taut, then snapped. The pig ran off trailing a ribbon of gut behind him.

JOHN BROWN. I have failed the cause of my century. Old man,

John Brown, be punished for your sin in this world and be punished in the next. I will embrace my punishment. I deserve it all.
KAGI. My Captain. (*The two men freeze as the lights fade on them and come up on Gov. Wise and the others, who unfreeze; Dr. Starry joins them.*)
GOV. WISE. Well, Doctor?
DR. STARRY. He will live.
LT. STUART. That is not possible. I myself stabbed him in the body several times and then, when my sword bent double, I hacked away at his skull. I surely crushed it.
COL. LEE. How could a heavy field sword bend double?
LT. STUART. I was wearing my lightweight, dress parade sword. When I stabbed him, it must have hit a buckle and bent.
COL. LEE. Why were you wearing a lightweight sword on active field duty?
LT. STUART. In my haste, sir, I grabbed the first sword that came into my hand.
GOV. WISE. And because of your haste that old man in there lives.
DR. STARRY. And will recover. . . . I must go now. There are many other wounded. (*He goes.*)
LT. STUART. I am sorry, sir.
HUNTER. "Sorry." What a lightweight word for so powerful a blunder. As lightweight as your dress parade sword.
COL. LEE. You may go. Dismissed. (*Lt. Stuart salutes. It is returned by Col. Lee. Lt. Stuart about faces and goes.*)
GOV. WISE. How clean, how convenient, if that old man had been killed. Now we will have to bring him to trial.
HUNTER. It is an open question as to whether his trial falls properly under the jurisdiction of Virginia or under the Federal Government.
GOV. WISE. We have him. We'll hold on to him. I will not risk trial in the Federal Courts.
COL. LEE. The first thing that old man did when he crossed the bridge was to seize Federal Government property. When captured, it was by United States troops on United States property.

HUNTER. When did his crime begin? When he crossed the bridge from Maryland into Virginia, or when he moved from Harpers Ferry into the Federal Armory?

COL. LEE. The jurisdiction for his trial is not as clear as you believe.

COL. WASHINGTON. If we do not manage this carefully, the North will transform him into a martyr with ten thousand people eager to dip their handkerchiefs in his blood.

GOV. WISE. (*Turning on Lee accusingly.*) If only your lieutenant had a heavy sabre in his hand instead of—

COL. LEE. (*Contemptuously.*) If only. If only.

HUNTER. This problem of jurisdiction can be thrashed out later. Let's get on with the interrogation! (*They start toward the Paymaster's Room. The two reporters come forward.*)

FIRST REPORTER. Gentlemen, you have asked us to stand aside while you confer privately. As newspaper reporters, we ask for permission to be present during the interrogation of John Brown.

GOV. WISE. Sorry. No time. Please leave.

COL. LEE. Governor Wise, with all due respect to your office and your person, you are standing on Federal Government property, and by the orders of the President of the United States of America, *I* have been put in charge here. The question of whether these reporters shall be present or not will be decided by John Brown himself. He is *my* prisoner and I shall offer him every courtesy.

COL. WASHINGTON. Col. Lee, as one Virginian to another, I implore you to reconsider.

COL. LEE. (*Formally, coldly.*) I will do my duty as I understand it.

HUNTER. (*With diplomacy.*) Naturally, Col. Lee, you must do your duty as you understand it. But I do wish you would be persuaded by Col. Washington.

COL. LEE. Sir, do not presume to instruct me in my duties. (*He turns his back on Hunter and goes toward John Brown and Kagi. He freezes.*)

GOV. WISE. (*To Col. Washington.*) Why object to having the reporters present?

COL. WASHINGTON. I urge you—try to dissuade Col. Lee.
GOV. WISE. Nonsense.
COL. WASHINGTON. John Brown was without food, water or sleep for forty hours. Yet he was able to discourse clearly with me on philosophic subjects throughout the night. His two sons were dying, his raid gone to smash, and though I tried to blunt his will to action, I did not succeed. Cut and bleeding and defeated though he is, I would not trust reporters in the same room with him.
GOV. WISE. I think you are overwrought.
COL. WASHINGTON. I have warned you. It is on your head. (*The characters freeze as the lights in this area dim and come up in the Paymaster's Room. John Brown and Kagi unfreeze. Col. Lee moves into the scene.*)
COL. LEE. Captain Brown, two newspaper reporters have requested permission to be present. It is for you to say whether I allow them in.
JOHN BROWN. Newspaper reporters? Let them come in.
COL. LEE. As you wish. (*He moves aside, out of the focus of the scene, and freezes.*)
JOHN BROWN. Lord, God, I swear to You, I will not fail my mission a second time. . . . Kagi, I have another chance!
KAGI. What?
JOHN BROWN. If God has seen fit to strike the sword from my hand, I will carry on the battle with the word. I will use the word—the word—and through it I will repair the disaster of the sword. (*The other characters unfreeze; all enter the room. The two reporters begin taking notes.*)
COL. LEE. Gentlemen, this is Captain Brown. Captain Brown, this is Governor Wise, Attorney Hunter. You have already met Col. Washington.
HUNTER. Captain Brown, who sent you?
JOHN BROWN. No man sent me here. It was my own prompting and that of my Maker—(*With profound wearniess, yet with fire.*)—or that of the Devil, whichever you please.
HUNTER. Did you come here under the auspices of the Northern Abolitionists?

JOHN BROWN. I came here under the auspices of John Brown.

HUNTER. But you did talk with the leaders of the Abolitionist movement about your expedition here?

JOHN BROWN. I decline to answer. I will not deny it; and I woud be a dunce to affirm it.

COL. LEE. (*Holding out some papers.*) These papers were found in your bag. They are a constitution and a table of military organization. Do you consider yours a military organization?

JOHN BROWN. I do.

COL. LEE. And you considered yourself the Commander-in-Chief of your military forces?

JOHN BROWN. I *am* Commander-in-Chief of that force.

COL. LEE. How large a force do you command?

JOHN BROWN. I have many supporters in the North and in the West.

COL. LEE. My question was how large a force did you command in your attack on Harpers Ferry?

JOHN BROWN. Men who were with me? Soldiers who bore arms?

COL. LEE. Yes, for the specific attack on Harpers Ferry.

JOHN BROWN. The total number of men who made the attack on Harpers Ferry, including myself—this total number was nineteen.

HUNTER. Captain Brown, there are reports of up to fiffteen hundred heavily armed men.

COL. LEE. Come, sir, I did not think you would stoop to lying. How many men had you with you? And where are they now?

JOHN BROWN. I value my word, sir. The total number of men who entered Harpers Ferry, including myself, was nineteen. (*Hunter, visibly perturbed, signals Gov. Wise, and the rest of his group to one side. The general lighting dims as the light comes up more brightly on this area.*)

HUNTER. (*To Col. Washington.*) Do you believe him? I must know your thought. If he is lying, then he is the spearhead of an invading host.

COL. WASHINGTON. And if he is not lying?

HUNTER. Then the world will soon know that nineteen men can shake the South to its roots. Answer me. Do you believe him?

COL. WASHINGTON. Yes. I believe him. He is a fanatic, but he is a man of truth and integrity. . . . Everything is clear to me now! I thought he had a large force dispositioned somewhere. It never occurred to me that he began his invasion with nineteen men.

COL. LEE. Don't glorify what happened in Harpers Ferry by calling it an invasion. It was a raid—a minor raid by nineteen poorly armed men.

COL. WASHINGTON. The men who have died on both sides of this relatively minor skirmish are the prelude to the men of the South and the men of the North who have yet to die. We are at war. We must recognize this fact of war and act upon this recognition.

COL. LEE. Let us continue our interrogation of that old man. (*As they move back into John Brown's area, the lights become uniform. John Brown is talking and the reporters are taking notes.*)

JOHN BROWN. How can any man enjoy his bread if there be others who have no bread? How can any man put his head on a pillow and sleep in peace if there be a man who has no pillow for his head?

FIRST REPORTER. But you can't take it upon yourself to correct every injustice. You can't bleed with every man who bleeds.

JOHN BROWN. Let my body bleed with the afflicted until there be no more afflicted. If every man against slavery were to feel that he, he, he, personally is responsible for the sin of slavery; that he alone must stand before the throne of God for the crime of turning a man into an animal, to be worked for profit like a horse, to be bred for profit like a bull—how long would slavery last? There would be a heaving and a fury in this land that would not be stilled until this crime against God and Man were swept away.

FIRST REPORTER. Then you consider yourself an instrument in the hands of Providence?

JOHN BROWN. I do.

COL. LEE. Upon what principle do you justify your acts?

JOHN BROWN. The Golden Rule. I pity the poor in bondage that have none to help them.

COL. LEE. The Golden Rule! Yet you took Col. Washington's horse and carriage.

JOHN BROWN. Have you yet to learn that we had a better right to them than Col. Washington had to his slaves? Is it a greater sin for me to take his horse when we are at war than it was for him to rob their mothers' cradles? Before God and high heaven, is there a law for one man that is not the law for every man? . . . Where are my poor and bleeding brothers and sisters? Can you tell? Am I not a man and their brother? . . . Be sure to report what I have said accurately.

GOV. WISE. Who let these reporters in? What are they doing here?

COL. WASHINGTON. I warned you.

JOHN BROWN. It is you who are the robbers. There are four million slaves in this country. You have robbed their wages for three hundred years, putting the proceeds in your pocket. If the hire of a man is worth but fifty cents profit a day, then you are robbing two million dollars a day from the least and the lonely and the last of my brothers and sisters. You have robbed the men of their wives, the wives of their husbands—and both of their children. You have turned them into beasts with the purpose of robbing them of their souls. Who then is the robber?

GOV. WISE. Captain Brown, the silver of your hair is reddened by the blood of crime. I suggest you shun these hard statements and think upon eternity.

JOHN BROWN. Whether my stay on earth will be 15 months, or 15 days, or 15 hours, I am equally prepared to go. I therefore tell you to be prepared; I am prepared.

GOV. WISE. Let us go.

COL. WASHINGTON. You have brought it on yourself.

HUNTER. (*To the reporters.*) Go along. (*They linger.*) Go along. You are here by courtesy.

FIRST REPORTER. Just one minute, please. (*To John Brown.*) If

you have anything further to say, I will report it faithfully.
JOHN BROWN. Say that I have not come here to act the part of robber, incendiary or ruffian. Say that the tears of the oppressed is my one reason for being here. Say furthermore unto the South, that it had better prepare itself for a settlement of this question—this Negro question, I mean—the end of that is not yet. (*The lights dim rapidly to blackout in the area of the Paymaster's Room. In the darkness, Kagi and the two reporters exit. Gov. Wise, Hunter, and the others move off to one side as the lights come up on their area.*)
SEN. MASON. Whether he is tried in Virginia or the Federal Courts, he will be found guilty and hanged. So why not throw the case into the lap of the Federal Government? Force *them* to do our work for us—force *them* to hang John Brown!
HUNTER. In a Federal Court he won't even come to trial until the spring term. You have heard the voice of John Brown. Can you afford to let it cry out that long? But if he is tried in Virginia, we can bring him to trial in a few days.
GOV. WISE. But who will prosecute John Brown? (*Pointing to Harding.*) Alcohol has turned his brain into a sponge.
COL. WASHINGTON. I know exactly the man to prosecute him. All that is necessary, Gov. Wise, is for you to appoint him special counsel for the State of Virginia.
GOV. WISE. Who?
COL. WASHINGTON. (*Indicates Hunter.*) Attorney Andrew Hunter.
HUNTER. You saw what happened when those two reporters were present. We had the law on our side, but still he was able to drag us into a position most unsavory. I have no desire to be dragged under by him.
COL. WASHINGTON. You are putting your narrow interests above that of the South. I had thought you to be a man of broader community spirit.
HUNTER. His trial will cast a long shadow—for that old man has begun a civil war. You are asking me to do something which may be very costly to me.

COL. WASHINGTON. Yes. It may be costly. But not as costly as the destruction of our slave economy. You recognize what John Brown recognizes: that the slave and the non-slave states are at war, a war now concealed but soon to be in the open. (*A small glow becomes visible in the sky. It grows, then bursts into angry color which is visible to the end of the scene.*)

GOV. WISE. What is that?

HUNTER. It is a barn on fire. I fear it is the first of many.

SEN. MASON. Look. There goes another.

COL. WASHINGTON. Our slaves have declared war on us. One part of our property burning the other part.

HUNTER. John Brown has set fire to the South. He is turning our foundations into ash.

COL. WASHINGTON. We are at war, gentlemen. It is folly and infatuation to accept any other premise. . . . I will get to John Floyd immediately. Even though Secretary of War, he is a Virginian first. He must arrange that the most modern arms are shipped to the southern arsenals—the older weapons to the North.

COL. LEE. Excuse me, gentlemen. I do not wish to participate, or even listen to such plans.

COL. WASHINGTON. You are a Virginian. Your own plantation lies less than one hundred miles from this spot. The value of your slaves has been diminished by John Brown's attack.

COL. LEE. True. My slaves have depreciated in value because of this raid. But I serve the Federal Government. I am an officer in the United States Army.

COL. WASHINGTON. What would be the conditions of your participation?

COL. LEE. My resignation from the United States Army. A most remote possibility.

COL. WASHINGTON. (*With rising impatience.*) Those barns are proof that you will not be able to continue this riding of two horses. Sooner or later you will be driven by your necessity.

COL. LEE. (*Coldly.*) By my necessity?

COL. WASHINGTON. (*The latent hostility of these two is in the open.*) Yes! That ferocious necessity which will drive you to make a choice. It will be one or the other—the Federal Government or the South. (*Col. Lee malevolently stares at Col. Washington and starts off.*)
HUNTER. Will you detail this conversation when you make out your military report?
COL. LEE. (*Stops and remains motionless. There is silence as he makes an important decision.*) No. My report will concern itself only with the military aspects of the raid.
HUNTER. Thank you. (*Col. Lee goes.*)
COL. WASHINGTON. (*With a smile.*) The first concession.
HUNTER. Excuse me, gentlemen. I have work to do.
COL. WASHINGTON. See to it you hang that Old Testament man!
HUNTER. I will get his conviction and he will hang. However, I warn you in advance. I will observe all the judicial decencies.
COL. WASHINGTON. By all means observe them—but at double-quick time.
HUNTER. (*Starts off, returns and stares at Charles Harding, whose snores cut the momentary stillness; roughly takes Harding's hair and jerks his head up.*) You drunken sot. You sleeping, snoring fool. (*Takes a glass of water and flings it viciously into Harding's face. He lets the head drop roughly as the lights fade on this area and come up on the courtroom in Charles Town, Virginia. A roll of drums is heard. This roll of drums will usher in and conclude all courtroom scenes. As Hunter moves into the scene from one side, John Brown is brought in on a stretcher from the other. His head is bandaged. Judge Parker is seated behind a bench.*)
JUDGE PARKER. Do you have counsel, or do you wish counsel to be appointed by the Court?
JOHN BROWN. I have sent for counsel. They have not yet arrived.
JUDGE PARKER. When will they come?
JOHN BROWN. I do not know. They are from the North. Perhaps in a few days.

HUNTER. We have no way of knowing if the lawyers received the message—or whether they will come, granting they did. Meanwhile, Virginia is in a state of unrest. May I, therefore, respectfully request that the Court appoint counsel for the defendant?

JUDGE PARKER. This Court will not yield to popular frenzy. But your other point is well taken. We have no way of knowing if counsel will arrive or when. (*He calls out.*) Mr. Botts. Mr. Dennis. Will you gentlemen please come forward? (*The men come forward.*) Will you serve as counsel for the defendant?

LAWSON BOTTS. I will serve.

THOMAS DENNIS. I will serve only if requested to—and then with reluctance.

JUDGE PARKER. Is the prisoner willing to accept?

JOHN BROWN. If I am to have a trial, I wish for counsel. But if I am to have nothing but the mockery of a trial, I care nothing about counsel.

JUDGE PARKER. Sir, you are to have a fair trial.

JOHN BROWN. I am a stranger here. I do not know the disposition or character of the two gentlemen named. I am sure they are honorable. But they have been born and raised in the South. Their whole cast of mind is alien to an understanding of why I marched on Harpers Ferry nine nights ago. I wish for my own counsel.

JUDGE PARKER. We have no way of knowing when your counsel will arrive—or, if your counsel will arrive. We must proceed.

JOHN BROWN. (*A sardonic bite in his voice.*) I wish for my own counsel. Do not hurry me to execution before they can reach me.

JUDGE PARKER. The prosecution will call its first witness.

JOHN BROWN. (*Rising from the stretcher with difficulty; with irony, which becomes contempt.*) Virginians, I did not ask to have my life spared at the time I was taken. If I am to be faced with a mere form—a trial for execution—spare yourselves the trouble. If you seek my blood you can have it at any moment without this mockery of a trial. (*He kneels on the stretcher.*)

JUDGE PARKER. Let the trial proceed. Mr. Hunter, call your first witness. (*The characters freeze as the lights fade quickly. A roll of drums. Hunter moves rapidly into playing area of Gov. Wise, Col. Washington and the others as lights come up on this area.*)

HUNTER. He is like quicksilver. I cannot grapple with him. I put my legal finger out to pin him down and he slithers away, coming up a moment later with an ethical position which leaves me winning the legal argument and he the moral. He lies on his stretcher, apparently unconcerned with what goes on around him, yet at exactly the right moment he rises up and makes a telling speech. And he is not speaking to the judge, jurors, nor even to the spectators in the courtroom. Through the reporters present, he speaks to the multitudes in the cities and the farmers in the fields. . . . He has done everything possible to delay the trial, so that it will have to be put over until the spring term. This I will not let happen. The trial will march from step to step, day by day, exactly as I have planned it. (*The roll of drums is heard.*) I must go back to the courtroom. (*Lights fade on this area as all characters freeze except Hunter. Light comes up on courtroom scene as Hunter moves into it.*)

BOTTS. Your Honor, my colleague and I wish to introduce evidence which has important bearing on this case. Even though the defendant has strictly enjoined us not to produce it, we go counter to his admonition. In the case of the State of Virginia versus John Brown, we enter a plea of strong suspicion of insanity. I present to the Court affidavits in good order which prove that insanity is hereditary on the maternal side of John Brown's family. (*He passes affidavits to Judge Parker.*) John Brown's grandmother, on his maternal side, was for six years hopelessly insane and died insane. The children of this grandmother, two uncles and two aunts of John Brown, were intermittently insane, and still another aunt died a hopeless lunatic. John Brown's only sister and one of his brothers are at intervals deranged. Six first cousins on the maternal side are afflicted with this terrible disease. A total of fourteen cases of insanity on the maternal side of John Brown's family. As for John Brown himself, can there be any question about his monomania regarding the subject of slavery? (*Hunter, with chagrin, throws his papers on the table.*)

JOHN BROWN. Yes. It is true. There is insanity on my mother's side of the family—as there is insanity in many families in this country. But I have escaped the taint and I will not allow you to inject the issue of my sanity in this trial. Try me on the crime for which I am charged! Either I will be declared innocent of the crime and be freed, or I will be declared guilty of the crime and be hanged. But you will not shatter the meaning of my life by declaring me insane. Try me on the issue! Try me on the issue! (*A roll of drums. Lights fade rapidly on this scene and come up on area of Gov. Wise, Col. Washington and the others. They unfreeze.*)

GOV. WISE. (*Reading a letter, one of several. He reads with exaggeration, achieving a touch of macabre humor.*) Governor Wise, Dear Sir. My two daughters have left with a party of women who propose to effect the rescue of John Brown. They number about sixteen, each wearing large petticoats filled with gunpowder having slow matches attached. If caught, they intend to set themselves off and, so effective is the inflammable material about them, that Virginia will be blown sky high. . . . If you find the girls, please send them back before they blow themselves up and many chivalrous gentlemen of Virginia along with them. Truly yours, An Anxious Father.

COL. WASHINGTON. The comic prelude to war.

GOV. WISE. Crank letters. Takes one's mind off the bitter hour.

HUNTER. (*Rushes in.*) He has done everything possible to delay the trial in order to carry it over into the spring term—and here it was handed to him, yet he refused it. Refused it. He will not allow a plea of insanity to be filed.

GOV. WISE. Should we not have him examined? If he were to be found insane—

HUNTER. He will not be found insane. If rational premises and consecutive reasoning, if memory and conception are evidence of a sound state of mind, then John Brown is sane. The question has been raised; let it becloud the issue. If we press for a conclusive answer, we will lose out.

SEN. MASON. Despite what you say, on the question of slavery, he *is* insane.

COL. WASHINGTON. If monomania is insanity, then he is insane. But then, so were Moses, Jesus, Mohammed and the whole host of social and religious reformers, for they too had a vision of Man on earth and pressed every means to achieve their vision. . . . If world opinion shifts and the institution of slavery is destroyed—(*Holding up a restraining hand.*)—and it very well might—

SEN. MASON. But the Bible gives sanction to slavery.

COL. WASHINGTON. We quote from the Bible to prove that slavery is a blessing approved by God. In the North, they advance as many quotations from the self-same Bible to prove that slavery is iniquitous. (*A messenger enters, gives Hunter a note, and goes.*)

HUNTER. (*Reading note.*) John Brown has just been brought in from his prison cell. I must return. (*A roll of drums. Lights fade on this area and come up on courtroom area as Hunter moves into it.*)

JUDGE PARKER. Have you anything to say before I pronounce sentence upon you?

JOHN BROWN. You have called me in suddenly. I did not expect to receive sentence until after the trial of Kagi and the other defendants. I am not prepared.

JUDGE PARKER. If you have something to say, it must be said at this time.

JOHN BROWN. This Court acknowledges the validity of the law of God. I see a book kissed, the Bible, which teaches the Golden Rule, that all things whatsoever I would that men should do to me, I should do even so to them. It teaches me, further, to remember them that are in bonds as bound with them. I endeavored to live up to that instruction. I believe that to have interfered in behalf of God's despised poor, I did not wrong, but right. Had I interfered in the manner which I admit, had I so interfered in behalf of the rich, the powerful, the intelligent, or any of that class, and suffered and sacrificed what I have in this interference, every man in this Court would have deemed it an act worthy of reward rather than punishment. And now, if it is deemed necessary that I should forfeit my life and mingle my blood with the blood of three of my sons and with the blood of millions in this slave country whose rights are disregarded by cruel and unjust laws, I say, let it be done. (*He looks about him. Then, gravely.*) I am now certain that the crimes of this guilty land will never be purged away but with a great outpouring of blood. I had hoped that my plan would do it without very much bloodshed. But my plan has gone down into the valley. I believe that now nought remains for this nation but the purge of blood.

JUDGE PARKER. John Brown, I pronounce the sentence of death. You are to be hanged on December 2nd, 1859, thirty days from today. And may God have mercy on your soul. (*Lights fade as the others move off and John Brown moves into scene of his prison cell in Charles Town, Virginia. Captain Avis ushers in Mary Brown. John Brown and Mary Brown stand apart at opposite ends of the cell; they do not go near each other until indicated.*)

CAPTAIN AVIS. Good afternoon, Captain Brown.

JOHN BROWN. Good afternoon, Captain Avis.

CAPTAIN AVIS. Mrs. Brown, my orders are that you are to leave here promptly at 9 o'clock this evening.

MARY. I understand.

CAPTAIN AVIS. The same military escort which conducted you to this jail will take you to a hotel. You are to remain in your room until after the hanging tomorrow morning.

MARY. I have agreed to it.

CAPTAIN AVIS. I must now ask you on your word of honor to assure me that you will not pass anything to your husband, that you will not give him message or information which can in any manner help him escape.

MARY. I have brought nothing into this cell except needle, thimble, thread and clothes brush.

CAPTAIN AVIS. Captain Brown, you have already given me your word.

JOHN BROWN. You know I would not walk out of this prison cell were the door open and a horse waiting for me. I am worth more to my cause dead than living. A few moments at the end of a rope will help me extract gain out of what appeared to be defeat. Would I not be a fool to walk out of that door?

CAPTAIN AVIS. I wish I could change the course of events tomorrow. . . . Captain Brown, Mrs. Brown, it is my duty to remain within earshot during your meeting.

MARY. (*With disappointment.*) Oh! Are we not to talk to each other in privacy?

CAPTAIN AVIS. Rest easy. I shall stand close enough to hear the sound of your voice—but far enough way to be unable to make out the words.

MARY. I thank you for your kindness, Captain Avis.

CAPTAIN AVIS. Speak in a low tone and you speak freely and in peace. (*Bowing to Mary Brown.*) Madam. (*He moves to a corner and stands with his back to the scene. The lights on this area gradually dim down so that his presence is muted. John Brown and Mary stand apart until Captain Avis has turned his back. Then they move toward each other. They study each other's faces.*)

MARY. Husband.

JOHN BROWN. Wife.

MARY. (*Looking at his scalp.*) Your wounds have not healed.

JOHN BROWN. Only these sword cuts on my head. A small matter. They will give me no trouble after tomorrow morning.

MARY. And your other wounds?

JOHN BROWN. They are healed.

MARY. Show me your other wounds. (*John Brown sits. Mary lifts the back of his shirt and studies his wounds. She kisses the three scars on his back. It is an act of devotion.*)

JOHN BROWN. Kiss my face, Mary Brown. (*They kiss. As she helps him stuff his shirt into his trousers, he says.*) When the young lieutenant slashed away at me, he could not crack open this hard nut of mine. (*He taps his head with his knuckles.*) It was the hand of God which guided the hand of the young lieutenant when he reached out for a sword—and thus I was kept alive to continue the fight until tomorrow morning.

MARY. Sit here. Let me have your jacket. It needs brushing and mending. (*John Brown takes off jacket and gives it to her. They sit. She sews and brushes during scene, as indicated.*)

JOHN BROWN. I do not mind dying. The bonds which have been holding me to this world are slowly loosening. I would rather die for my cause than merely pay my debt to nature as we all must do eventually.

MARY. I accept what you say.

JOHN BROWN. For a lifetime I fought, and God let me fight until that moment in Harpers Ferry when He took the sword out of my hand. But in that same moment, He gave me the sword of the spirit. Mary, it is a surprise to me that the sword of the spirit is a thousand times the stronger.

MARY. God's plan was better than yours, else He would have let you keep your own.

JOHN BROWN. (*With grief.*) But in myself I am disappointed! What a blunder to stay on when the military situation began to go against me. Why did I not leave at once and go into the mountains?

MARY. If Samson had not told Delilah wherein lay his great strength, would he have been able to pull down the temple of the Philistines?

JOHN BROWN. I believe that nothing I have suffered or may yet suffer will be lost to the cause of God or Man. I believe this. I know it. But I ask—I ask—when—when does the servant of God and His partner, when does God's human partner learn the full intention of God, so that he can serve humbly *but* with more intelligence? (*After a pause, answering his own question.*) It seems only at the final instant of unfolding. . . . Sometimes it is difficult to travel in faith; it requires great courage to be a partner of God.

MARY. (*Giving him his jacket.*) Put on your jacket. (*He does.*) What shirt will you wear tomorrow? (*He points to it. She examines it and begins to sew.*) Some buttons are loose.

JOHN BROWN. Mary, I very much would prize a little history of your success or failure on the farm.

MARY. We have had a fair crop of hay. We will have enough to feed the cow and horse until we let them out for spring pasture.

JOHN BROWN. That's good about the hay. It would be ruinous to buy hay in late winter.

MARY. The peas have failed almost entirely. But there is a good bean crop, and we have potatoes and turnips and some carrots. We will manage the winter.

JOHN BROWN. You always have. Thank you for your history.

MARY. Now I have a question to ask of you. Why did you refuse to allow me to visit you three weeks ago even though I had Governor Wise's permission to do so? And why did you not want me to come today?

JOHN BROWN. Because of the expense. (*In answer to her look.*) This trip will use up the little money you have to buy flour for bread, to buy clothing for the children and you through the winter.

MARY. What of the comfort of our meeting again?

JOHN BROWN. It will be dearly paid for by the pain of our coming separation at 9 o'clock.

MARY. Since I cannot have one without the other, I am prepared to take them together.

JOHN BROWN. Mary, I hear stories, but I cannot get accurate information. What has happened to the bodies of Oliver and Watson?

MARY. What have you heard?

JOHN BROWN. The students from a nearby medical school robbed Watson's body from the grave and dissected it. Is it true? (*There is a silence.*) Speak the truth. Don't withhold it.

MARY. They took the skin off his body and varnished it. Now there is a dispute. Some want to keep it as it is, varnished; others want to stuff it and send it on exhibition to fairs and circuses; still others want to cut up the skin and make hunting pouches to be sold as souvenirs.

JOHN BROWN. And what has happened to Oliver's body?

MARY. They took Oliver's body and that of Newby and wrapped their arms about each other as though in embrace, chest to chest and face to face, and dropped them into a common grave. . . . Did they think to desecrate the mortal remains of our son by burying him with a Negro? What fools they are, to think their degradation can be ours. My son is sanctified. . . . Weep not for me, oh daughters of Jerusalem; weep for yourselves and for your sons.

JOHN BROWN. Mary, try to build up the broken walls of our once great family and make the utmost of every stone that is left.

MARY. I will build the wall again. . . . And your body?

JOHN BROWN. I do not think you will get it. Virginia will want to hold on to it. But do not grieve. It makes but little difference what is done with it.

MARY. No. Your body is to be delivered to me. I wrote to Governor Wise. He granted my request. Here is the order.

JOHN BROWN. (*Reads the paper.*) That is very chivalrous of him.

MARY. I will bring your body to the farm where you will be buried.

JOHN BROWN. Mary, think of the expense. This money must be used for you and the children, not for the dead.

MARY. I will take your body to our farm and you will be buried there. That is the way it will be.

JOHN BROWN. If that is the way it will be, then bury me in the shadow of the granite rock.

MARY. I will put you in the shadow of the rock.

JOHN BROWN. Mary, Mary, so often in the watches of the night I longed to be back at the farm with you and the children—to be husband and father. Instead, how many times I have gone away, sometimes for half a year at a time, and returned briefly to go away again, leaving you with the care of the farm and the raising of the children—and often another babe on the way.

MARY. Have I ever complained?

JOHN BROWN. The children needed a father; I was not there. My wife needed a husband; I was not there.

MARY. Have you ever heard me utter one word of protest?

JOHN BROWN. We were young once. But the days of our years have passed and now we are gray. And now there are no more days.

MARY. No. Not a single word further. You said that in the still watches of the night you longed to be back at the farm with me and the children. In those same still watches I would ask myself, what did I do to deserve the glory of being your wife. In all our married years, not even for a single hour, would I be anyone else but what I am—Mary Brown, wife of John Brown.

JOHN BROWN. Even tonight?

MARY. (*Fiercely.*) Especially tonight. I would not be any place tonight but where I am. (*They cling to one another. The lights come up on Captain Avis. He turns and moves toward them. Mary moves away from John Brown.*) It's time?

CAPTAIN AVIS. (*Nods. Then.*) I have been praying through the night that the soul of your husband will not be damned.

JOHN BROWN. Look into my face. Do you doubt that before this day is over I will stand before the throne of God?

CAPTAIN AVIS. I know that you will stand before the throne of God. (*He turns and, with Mary following, exits. The beat of drums. The lights dim to blackness.*)

THE END

LORENA

D7 G D7 G G7 C D7 G
1. The years creep slow - ly by, Lo - re - na, The snow is on the grass a - gain; The
2. A hun - dred months have passed, Lo - re - na, Since last I held that hand in mine, And
3. We loved each oth - er then, Lo - re - na, More than we ev - er dared to tell; And
4. The sto - ry of that past, Lo - re - na, A - las! I care not to re - peat, The
5. Yes, these were words of thine, Lo - re - na, They burn with - in my mem - 'ry yet; They
6. It mat - ters lit - tle now, Lo - re - na, The past is in the 'ter - nal past; Our
G7 C D7
sun's low down the sky, Lo - re - na, The frost gleams where the flowers have
felt the pulse beat fast, Lo - re - na, Though mine beat fast - er far than
what we might have been, Lo - re - na, Had but our lov - ings pros - pered
hopes that could not last, Lo - re - na, They lived, but on - ly lived to
touched some ten - der chords, Lo - re - na, Which thrill and trem - ble with re -
heads will soon lie low, Lo - re - na, Life's tide is ebb - ing out so
G Solo Voice: Em Am(6) B7
Hum
been. But the heart throbs on as warm - ly now, As
thine. A hun - dred months was flow - ery May, When
well But then, 'tis past, the years are gone, I'll
cheat. I would not cause e'en one re - gret To
gret. 'Twas not thy wo - man's heart that spoke; Thy
fast. There is a fu - ture, o, thank God! Of
B7 Em All: D7 G G7
when the sum - mer days were nigh; Oh! the sun can nev - er dip so
up the hil - ly slope we climbed, To watch the dy - ing of the
not call up their shad - ow - y forms; I'll say to them, "Lost years,
ran - kle in your bos - om now; For "if we try we may sleep
heart was al - ways true to me: A du - ty, stern and press - ing,
life this is so small a part! 'Tis dust to dust be - neath the
C D7 G
low, A - down af - fec - tion's cloud - less sky.
day, And hear the dis - tant church bells chime.
on! Sleep on! nor heed life's pelt - ing storms.
get." Were words of thine long years a - go.
broke. The tie which linked my soul with thee.
sod. But there, up there 'tis heart to heart.